"GOD'S HONORABLE MENTIONS"

Jim Cole-Rous

For information write: Rev. Jim Cole-Rous
3134 Maranatha Ln., # 34, Springfield MO 65803

ISBN:1494247461
ISBN-13:9781494247461

DEDICATION

This book is dedicated to the memory of Dr. John
Garlock, my mentor at South African Bible Institute, David
Newington who encouraged me to excel in study of the Holy
Scriptures
My esteemed friend William F. P. Burton,
a pioneer missionary to the Congo,
who graced my home the last three winters of his life
and opened my mind to do greater things
than I dreamed for God.

James Cole-Rous,
Springfield MO
2013

INTRODUCTION

It is my belief that when the Holy Spirit leads an inspired writer to record someone's name in the Bible, there is a story of courage and tenacity; or infamy and duplicity that we can learn from.

In November of 1966 I spent some weeks in the land of the Bible. One day I traveled to Emmaus where Jesus appeared to two disciples on the day of His resurrection. Above the entrance to the Church I noticed a bas relief portraying the supper with Jesus between the two disciples. What I saw there drove me to restudy the story of the resurrection; and I was able to establish just who the 'other' disciple was.

That was the beginning of what now forty-four years later has become a passion to share the story behind the story, of these men and women of faith. Over the last four years I have researched the scriptures, and writings of great commentators, to find the background and relationships of these people whose names are often lightly passed over in the reading of the book of books.

For the sake of helping you keep track of relationships, I have attempted to present each person in this book in chronological order, as far as is possible. I have had to go beyond the pages of scripture to find some information about these people, but I have done so cautiously, giving due consideration to the source from which my information was derived.

My wish is that you may be informed and encouraged as you read of the trials and triumphs of these very human people who happened to live and be involved in God's account of the great work of reconciliation of the lost to Himself.

Jim Cole-Rous

James Cole-Rous is Director of Content for Network211.com's Global Christian Center web site. He is Managing Editor for the Ozarks Chapter of American Christian Writers, and a regular contributor to The Way.co.uk, subscription-service daily devotional; published in the United Kingdom.

CONTENTS

ACKNOWLEDGMENTS

Cover Illustration by Peter Dell Copyright © 2012
Cover design by Peter Dell, Network211.com

Book Title: courtesy of Anita Jaeger, Orland Park, Illinois.
Editing by Director of Content, Network 211.com

Research for the articles required extensive fact checking.
Quotations have been used in terms of the 'Fair Usage' provisions
of the Copyright act. Every effort has been made to include
sources from which the extra-biblical information was found. This
work comprises four years of study and research.

The Bible has been the author's first reference; writers of Biblical
commentaries have been carefully studied, and where any
commentator has departed from the actual account found
in the scriptures, he has chosen not to quote from that source.

The writings of the Church Fathers and the Rabbins
have been referenced with the same standards of priority by the
author. More weight has been given to accounts that have more
than one source, as long as neither contradicts Holy Writ.

1 WHO WAS MELCHIZEDEK?

For this Melchizedek, king of Salem, priest of God Most High, who met Abraham returning from the slaughter of the kings and blessed him, to whom also Abraham divided a tenth part of all (being first, by interpretation, King of righteousness, and then also King of Salem, which is King of peace; without father, without mother, without genealogy, having neither beginning of days nor end of life, but made like unto the Son of God), abideth a priest continually. Now consider how great this man was, unto whom Abraham, the patriarch, gave a tenth out of the chief spoils. And they indeed of the sons of Levi that receive the priest's office have commandment to take tithes of the people according to the law, that is, of their brethren, though these have come out of the loins of Abraham: but he whose genealogy is not counted from them hath taken tithes of Abraham, and hath blessed him that hath the promises. But without any dispute the less is blessed of the better." Hebrews 7:1-7

The Biblical account of Melchizedek makes one thing very clear, he was extremely old, so much so that no one seemed to know his genealogy. It also shows Abraham recognized this 'great man' as a Priest of the most high God, and gave him the tenth part of his spoils of victory over Amraphel king of Shinar, Arioch king of Ellasar, Chedorlaomer king of Elam, and Tidal king of Goiim, (Gen 14:1) the rulers of the lands we know today as Iran, Iraq and Syria.

The word Melchizedek is not a person's name but a title.

This is interpreted in Heb. 7:2 as "king of righteousness". He is also said to be 'king of Salem' meaning king of the city of Peace. So we have a man whose personal name is not yet revealed to us.

There is a further consideration. Hebrews 7: 3 says he was made like unto the 'Son of God'. Now in Luke 3:38 Adam is said to be the 'Son of God'.

So we begin to wonder if this Priest of the Most High God was a direct descendant of Adam through Noah. We have a very careful chronology of Noah's offspring, and it is clearly evident that one of them, Ham was cursed through his son Canaan. He was not considered righteous. The Genesis account in chapter 11, records the building of the Tower of Babel and God's judgment upon them. Then no further notice is made of Japheth, but Genesis takes up the story of God's dealings with Noah's first-born Shem. Could he still be alive in the time of Abraham? In the book of Genesis there are people listed who lived close to 1,000 years. I began to do an overlay of the lives of the first few generations and was amazed to find that the life span of Adam and Noah's father Lamech, overlapped by 56 years. Noah's grandfather, Methuselah, lived 243 years of his life concurrently with Adam.

Shem, Noah's firstborn son, was alive for the last 99 years of Methuselah's life, and would have heard many stories from his great grandfather about the creation and the story of Adam and Eve.

Gen 11:10-11 is interesting:

"These are the generations of Shem. Shem was a hundred years old, and begat Arpachshad two years after the flood: and Shem lived after he begat Arpachshad five hundred years, and begat sons and daughters".

Shem was 600 years old when he died, having lived 500 of them after the flood. My studies of the offspring of Shem indicate that he outlived all of his immediate family.

Abraham was born 292 years after the flood. Shem lived another 208 years after Abraham's birth. Abraham dies 467 years after Flood at which time Shem was 567 years old and lived 33 more years after the death of Abraham, and may have been present at Abraham's funeral!

The 'Book of the Bee', written in the thirteenth century, by Solomon of Akhlat, Bishop of the Nestorian Church of the East in Basrah, Iraq, is a collection of stories and beliefs then held by the Jewish community in Iraq. Bishop Solomon records the story with many details; from which I have extracted the essence:

"When Noah died, he commanded Shem concerning the bones of Adam, for they were with them in the ark, . . . Shem went by night into the ark, and took Adam's coffin; and he sealed up the ark, saying to his brethren, 'My father commanded me that no one should go into it . . . And he journeyed by night with the angel before him . . . until they came and stood upon the spot where our Lord was crucified.

"When he was old, the kings of the earth heard his fame, and eleven of them gathered together and came to see him; and they entreated him to go with them, but he would not be persuaded.

When he did not conform to their wishes, they built a city for him there, and he called it Jerusalem; and the kings said to one another, 'This is the king of all the earth, and the father of nations.' When Abraham came back from the battle of the kings, he passed by the mount of Jerusalem; and Melchizedek came forth to meet him, and Abraham made obeisance to Melchizedek, and gave him tithes of all that he had with him. Melchizedek embraced him and blessed him, and gave him bread and wine from that which he was wont to offer up as an offering." (Book of the Bee. edited and translated by. Earnest A. Wallis Budge, M.A. [Oxford, the Clarendon Press 1886]. Wikipedia)

Jewish tradition holds that Melchizedek was keeper of the grave of Adam on Mt. Moriah. Golgotha even in Jesus day was called "The Place of the Skull". Melchizedek in Scripture is likened to a Son of God (i.e. direct descendant of Adam). Abraham recognized Melchizedek's superiority as a Priest and tithed to him. It seems that Melchizedek was really Shem, the first born son of Noah.

This being so, the Genesis account was not a garbled fable handed down through many generations, but the true account that was passed from Adam to Abraham, with only two intermediaries; Methuselah and Shem!

2 DINAH THE DAUGHTER OF LEAH

How she was raised:

*H*ow she was raised:
She was Dinah the Daughter of Leah, born to Jacob in Haran (Gen 46:7). This happened about a year before the birth of Joseph to Rachel. She was therefore about seven years of age when Jacob contracted with Laban for stock, to provide for his own house, and about five more years passed, ten lambing seasons, before Joseph left Haran to return to Canaan. Thus we find Dinah about 12 to 13 years of age as they entered Canaan. Dinah's brothers Simeon and Levi were therefore about 17 and 14 respectively, while Joseph would have been a year or so younger than her.

Jacob had covenanted with God that he would return to Bethel; to make that place God's house indeed (Gen 28:22). Now they were finally on their way southwards, but the old trade route leads from the river crossing where Jacob wrestled with God, later called Mahanaim, through the flue plain of Mukhna stretching from N. to S. to the city of Shechem, situated on the continental divide between the mountains of Gerizim and Ebal. Here the rich black soil was watered by fountains that produced abundant Olive groves, fruit orchards and vegetables. Here was rich grazing available for his flocks. Jacob negotiated with the King of Shechem and bought property. He stayed there for nearly three years, instead of moving on to Bethel.

How she was raped:

Josephus relates that every spring a festival celebrating the fertility of life was held, and the women of Shechem danced (Josephus-Ant 1:21). This was just too attractive to the girl Dinah, now about 16 years of age, and she went out to 'see the daughters of the land'. Her brothers were at work in the fields and she was seen by the son of King Hamor of Shechem.

Prince Shechem decided to take her and keep her for his own. He raped her, but also fell in love with her and decided to make her his wife.

'Abduction Marriage' was common in that culture and time, and he implored his father to negotiate and formalize the marriage with Jacob and his family. There were two problems that outraged the family. First the forcible rape and humbling of their sister and second the possibility in the Canaanite culture that when Shechem tired of her she would be moved to the 'Harem' with his concubines, and replaced with another wife. The truth was that the children of Abraham were not willing to form marriages outside of the tribe.

When Hamor and Shechem came to meet with Jacob and Dinah's brothers, Simeon and Levi, they suggested circumcision as a way the marriage and intermingling of the Canaanites and the family of Jacob could be accomplished. They knew they were not strong enough to withstand the Shechemites at that moment and needed to buy some time.

How she recovered:

Hamor and Shechem returned to the City and persuaded the people to comply with the Hebrews' demands; insinuating that they would ultimately own all of what the Hebrews possessed. Once the men of Shechem were circumcised, the sons of Jacob took their opportunity to attack the city on the third day while the feverish pain was at its worst, and kill every man in it, and rescue their sister from the palace. Seduction is still punished by death among the Arab peoples today, and usually carried out by the brothers of the girl who had been raped. It is termed an 'Honor Killing'.

Hamor and Shechem were killed, along with all the other men of the town, but the neighboring peoples became threatening, and Jacob had no choice but to move away from there. Sometime after that the family realized that Dinah was pregnant. She gave birth nine months later to a boy they named Shaul (Gen. 46:10). Technically Dinah was now a widow whose deceased husband Shechem was a Canaanite so she is referred to as the 'Canaanitish woman'.

How she was restored:

Dinah's Brother Simeon took her into his household as a protected widow, and adopted her son Shaul, also spelled Saul, the child thus obtained an inheritance in Israel (Gen 46:10). When Isaac died Jacob and his brother Esau performed the burial rites (Gen 35:29). They had been reconciled after Jacobs return. Esau had become a strong ruler over Edom, ruling from the city of Seir, that we know today as Petra.

6

Some years later Jacob, hearing that Joseph was still alive, moved all the family to Egypt, and Dinah went with them as part of Simeon's household. (Gen 46:15).

Now the esteemed Rabbi Rashi (Rabbi Shlomo Yitzhak), who lived in the 15th century, writes that Dinah was married to Job; after Job's recovery from the sickness and disaster that also took the life of his first wife Sitidos.

Job, also called Jobab, lived the land of Uz, called Ausitis, and is listed as a King of Edom (Gen 36:31-33). His friends in Job 42:9 were Eliphaz (Gen36:10), Bildad the Shuhite and Zophar the Naamathite (Gen 25:2, 6,). According to the Septuagint, Zophar was king of the Minaites. He most probably came from that Naamah, which was bordering upon the Edom to the south.

Here are Albert Barnes' Notes on Job in the Bible: (Gen 34:1-34 Barnes Notes – Dinah's Dishonor) this is translated out of a Syrian book.

"He dwelt indeed in the land of Ausitis, on the confines of Idumea and Arabia. His first name was Jobab; and having married an Arabian woman, he had by her a son whose name was Ennon. He was himself a son of Zare, one of the sons of Esau; and his mother's name was Bosorra; so that he was the fifth in descent from Abraham. And these were the kings who reigned in Edom, over which country he also bore rule. The first was Balak, the son of Beor, and the name of his city was Dannaba. After Balak, Jobab, who is called Job; . . . And the friends who came to him were Eliphaz of the sons of Esau, the king of the Thaimanites; Bildad, the sovereign of the Saueheans; and Zophar, the king of the Manaians."

While there is no further comment in the Bible on Dinah, there are many allusions in the Septuagint and rabbinical writings to the second marriage of Job, or King Jobab, to Dinah, and if this be the case the closing verses of Job 42:12-13 would apply to Dinah as well!

"So the LORD blessed the latter end of Job more than his beginning: for he had fourteen thousand sheep, and six thousand camels, and a thousand yoke of oxen, and a thousand she asses. He had also seven sons and three daughters."

3 JOSEPH'S PORTION

I f there is one thing that families find difficult to accept, it is the discovery that they have not received what they expected; when the Lawyer reads the Will of their recently deceased relative. Often bitterness and jealousy become dominant in the minds and hearts of the siblings and relatives involved.

Jesus was implored to intervene in the case of a man who felt he had not been fairly endowed in the settlement of an estate. Interestingly, Jesus refused to arbitrate the matter. When someone dies, they have the right to decide what and how much of their estate would go to those left behind.

We have certain expectations, based upon our ethnic culture and world view. In Bible times it was no different. The custom was that the first born son would be given a double share of the estate. Whatever the case, it is usually the ones that get a lesser or no share that become hostile and wish to contest the Will!

When the Patriarch, Jacob called Joseph and the rest of his brothers together for what appeared to be the declaration of his last wishes, we find Joseph coming to the Old Man's bedside, accompanied by his two sons, Manasseh and Ephraim. I have seen pictures, in Children's Bibles of the scene by ill-informed artists who show Joseph as about 30 years old with the two little boys, perhaps 5 and 6 years in appearance. Reader, dispossess yourself of that idea. Joseph was 30 years of age when he took the position of Pharaoh's right hand man. He had 2 sons born within the first 7 years before the famine began, and it was nine years after his coming to power that his brothers and father arrived in Egypt (Gen. 45:6).

When Joseph introduced his father to the Pharaoh King of Egypt, Jacob told the King his age, as being 130 years of age (Gen. 47:9).

Jacob died 17 years later, at the age of 147 (Gen. 47:28) so his grand-sons Manasseh and Ephraim were a minimum 19 years of age, and probably about 24 and 25. Joseph was 56 at the time of Jacob's death.

Now they approach Jacob who summoned his strength to sit up, and make some very startling declarations concerning their inheritance. He first offers to speak a blessing over the young men, and accompanies this with the simultaneous laying on of hands. Joseph knowing the custom, positions Manasseh his oldest boy to be under the Patriarch's right hand, and Ephraim, the younger under the left hand. Then Jacob, who is virtually blind, crosses his arms and gives the greater blessing to the younger, in spite of Joseph's protest.

There is an interesting footnote in the Amplified bible concerning this:

"Gen 48:14: God acts independently of the claims of priority based on time of birth when He chooses men. He too "crossed His hands" in the case of Seth whom He chose over Cain; of Shem over Japheth; of Isaac over Ishmael; of Jacob over Esau; of Judah and Joseph over Reuben; of Moses over Aaron; of David over all his brothers; and of Mary over Martha".

We need to understand that human customs and expectations are not to be imposed on God!

Now Jacob tells Joseph that he is adopting Manasseh and Ephraim as his own; in place of Joseph. The old man had disinherited Reuben, his first-born, for sinful conduct. Now he replaces Joseph in favor of his two boys, thus making up the number of his tribes to twelve again. He also gives the blessing of the first-born to Ephraim, the younger of the two (Gen. 48:19).

The question now is, "Where does that leave Joseph?"

Jesus himself provides the answer. In John 4:5 we read that Jacob gave Joseph a portion of land in Israel. This portion of land was in the district of Shechem (Gen. 48:22). Joseph had lived there as a teenager, and went there initially searching for his brothers just before he was sold to the Midianites as a slave (Gen 33:18; 37:12). Today you can visit Israel and see Jacob's well. I have been there and drunk of the cold refreshing water from it myself.

Jacob had owned the land, and lost it to the Amorites, and then at a later time he recovered it; and kept the title to it. Joseph never got to see the property again after having stayed there a short while, as a boy with his Father and brothers, but it became his inheritance, and that of his other children and their descendants.

Joseph, in his dying moments, made them swear an oath that when God delivered them from Egypt, they would take his body with them (Gen. 50:25-26). He died more than 350 years before Israel left Egypt!

Moses and the Children of Israel obeyed that command and carried that Sarcophagus around for 40 years until they took possession of the land or promise. Joshua was able to bury Joseph's body in that parcel of ground in Shechem (Joshua 24:32).

This was a supreme act of faith by a man who had firmly believed the dreams and promises of God as a boy, and still trusted the Lord in his old age. This act of faith is mentioned as an example to the believer in Hebrews 11:22.

For a Christian, here is a valuable lesson. You do not always get what you think you deserve as you walk this vale of tears, but God never forgets your labor of love for Him. He has promised you an inheritance with the saints of light (Col. 3:24, 1 Pet. 1:4).

When you keep Eternity in view, you will not fret about what is going on around you. You will have the peace and joy of God in your heart. Like Joseph, you need to hold on to the dreams that God has imbedded in your heart. Be faithful regardless of the circumstances, and let God work out His perfect plan for your life.

You too are headed for the Promised Land if you walk by Faith!

4 WHAT HAPPENED TO ORPAH?

It was spring time when Ruth and Orpah stood on the road leading from Moab, east of the Dead Sea, to Bethlehem in Judea. Naomi their Jewish mother-in-law bade them farewell. She was destitute, her husband and two sons deceased. The girls were Moabites; foreigners to the people of Israel.

Naomi had nothing to offer them, and suggested they return to their mother's house until they could find new husbands. When the girls protested, and said they would follow her, Naomi knew that they could not find acceptance unless they became believers in the One True God of Israel. Ruth made her confession of faith in Jehovah God (Ruth 1:4–14), but her sister Orpah decided to stay, and turned back.

The name Orpah means 'the nape of the neck'. This was a polite way of naming the woman who had turned her back on her mother-in-law of ten years. Orpah had figured out that she could do better by returning to her mother's house, for her mother was the Queen, married to Eglon the Moabite King. Princesses did not have to die of hunger as widows in a foreign land!

The daughters of Eglon had married the sons of Elimelech, a wealthy prince of Judah, and son of Salmon. He had been driven by famine from Bethlehem, and made a politically advantageous marriage for his sons, forming an alliance with the King of Moab After the death of Elimelech and his sons, there was nothing left for the widow except the family property in Bethlehem[1]

.

---

[1]www.jewishvirtuallibrary.org/jsource/judaica/ejud_0002_0015_0_152 18.html.

In those times the land remained the possession of the family, and was like a life insurance policy to a widow.

We know that Ruth became the Great-Grandmother of King David 3, and her name is found the line of Jesus' ancestors; but what happened to Orpah?

The Jewish Rabbins tell us in the Aggadah that the real name of Orpah was Harafu[2]. She did find a new husband; the result of a shrewd political alliance between Eglon King of Moab and the Philistine King of Gath. In those days there were still giants living in Moab, but most of them had moved to the Coastal plain (Joshua 15:14), and Orpah became the wife of one of these 'Eminem', or giants. She bore him four very big boys. Their names were Ishbibenob, Saph (2 Sam 21:16-18), Lahmi and Goliath (1 Chron 20:5).

When her boys were of full age and mature fighters, Goliath challenged the army of Israel, and was killed by young David; his great grandmother Princess Ruth was sister to Harafu whom we call Orpah. David was challenged in subsequent battles by the brothers of Goliath, until all of them were killed by the leaders of David's army. Orpah was an aged woman when Abishai, a general in David's Army, attacked Ishbibenob. She tried to hinder Abishai from killing her son, and died in the effort.

2

www.jewishvirtuallibrary.org/jsource/judaica/ejud_0002_0015_0_1521 8.html

14

5 AGAG KING OF THE AMALEKITES

First Biblical Mention of the Amalekites
"And Timna was concubine to Eliphaz Esau's son; and she bare to Eliphaz Amalek: these were the sons of Adah Esau's wife." Genesis 36:12. In Genesis we encounter the first Amalek, son of Eliphaz, who was the son of Esau by Timna, Esau's concubine. These details make it clear that there was no title or inheritance in Israel entailed to either Eliphaz or his descendant, Amalek.

Opposition by Amalekites to Israel

Exodus 17:8-9 "Then came Amalek, and fought with Israel in Rephidim. And Moses said unto Joshua, Choose us out men, and go out, fight with Amalek: tomorrow I will stand on the top of the hill with the rod of God in mine hand."

Exodus 17:14-16 "And the LORD said unto Moses, Write this for a memorial in a book, and rehearse it in the ears of Joshua: for I will utterly put out the remembrance of Amalek from under heaven. And Moses built an altar, and called the name of it Jehovahnissi: For he said, 'Because the LORD hath sworn that the LORD will have war with Amalek from generation to generation'".

As the people of Israel left Egypt, the very first battle they were forced into, was instigated by the Amalekites. God delivered them, as we read in Exodus. Amalek was beaten, not destroyed. They would come back again.

Initial Mention of Agag as King of the Amalekites.

"He shall pour the water out of his buckets, and his seed shall be in many waters, and his king shall be higher than Agag, and his kingdom shall be exalted." Numbers 24:7

"And he took Agag the king of the Amalekites alive, and utterly destroyed all the people with the edge of the sword. But Saul and the people spared Agag," 1 Samuel 15:8-9.

God had specifically ordered the destruction of the Amalekites, through the Prophet Samuel.

King Saul did not carry out the orders he received, and made excuse that he had brought some of the best cattle to use in sacrifices. Of course when sacrifices were made to God, the people got to enjoy eating the meat that was cooked! King Agag was also spared by Saul, but Samuel had Agag executed. God intended that the destruction of the Amalekites be His judgment on them, but Saul was looking to see how his men could benefit from the plunder. Samuel makes it clear that God is more interested in our obedience than our self-satisfaction.

Meaning of the Name Agag

The name in Arabic means, to "Burn". It is not a person's name but his title, as Pharaoh is a title of the Kings of Egypt. This was the 'Flame' that would lead his nation to attack and burn Israel repeatedly. David, was given the City of Ziklag, by the King Achish; and while he and his troops followed the Philistines going to war against King Saul, the Amalekites came and burned Ziklag to the Ground.

"And it came to pass, when David and his men were come to Ziklag on the third day, that the Amalekites had invaded the south, and Ziklag, and smitten Ziklag, and burned it with fire;" 1 Samuel 30:1

This was the methodology of the Agagite Kings of the Amalekites, whose title was the 'Flame' or the 'Burning One'. They warred with a 'Scorched Earth Policy'.

We encounter an Agagite hostile to Israel

"After these things did king Ahasuerus promote Haman the son of Hammedatha the Agagite, and advanced him, and set his seat above all the princes that were with him."

Esther 3:1 "And the king took his ring from his hand, and gave it unto Haman the son of Hammedatha the Agagite, the Jews' enemy." Esther 3:10

The history of the feud between the Amalekites and Israel continued for many hundreds of years. They were the first to attack Israel as they exited Egypt. They attacked Israel repeatedly over the years of the Judges.

King Saul was commanded to annihilate the entire tribe: man, woman and child, livestock and all that pertained to them. His disobedience ultimately cost him his throne. Still there were remnants of Amalekites who were living elsewhere and survived, and regrouped. One of them was Haman, the son of Hammedatha, of the Royal blood of Amalek, who was Esau's grandson.

Haman was captured during the Persian conquest of Egypt, and taken to Shushan, the Palace of Xerxes. Here he hatched a plan to exterminate all the Jews in what was then the greatest federation of nations in the world.

The old enmity remained, but God used Queen Esther to foil the plot and save the nation of Israel from the Amalekite, Haman.

"And [Esther] said, If it please the king, and if I have found favor in his sight, and the thing seem right before the king, and I be pleasing in his eyes, let it be written to reverse the letters devised by Haman the son of Hammedatha the Agagite, which he wrote to destroy the Jews which are in all the king's provinces:" Esther 8:5

The Jews still commemorate this deliverance in the yearly Festival of Purim, on the 14th and 15th of Adar (February, March). Looking at the historical timeline, it is amazing to see that the enmity fostered between Jacob and Esau, festered for some 1,700 years within the Biblical record until 300 B.C. when Alexander the Great fought and conquered Ahasuerus - Xerxes.

When people are in a covenant relationship with God, He takes care of them, as His own special people. Have you come to the place where the Lord is your Shepherd, King and Savior? You can come into that relationship now, for God loved you so much He sent His only son into the world to pay for you to be reconciled to God through what He did for you on the Cross of Calvary. No matter who seems against you, if you belong to the Lord God, you will find He will never leave your, or desert you.

6 THE ETHIOPIAN WOMAN!

Then Miriam and Aaron spoke against Moses because of the Ethiopian woman whom he had married; for he had married an Ethiopian woman" Numbers 12:1

Hebrew: kushiyth (Koo-sheeth') a Cushite woman. (Strong's Hebrew Dictionary)

The sister and brother challenge Moses about his wife. They follow up this with a challenge to his leadership. Adam Clarke comments: Num 12:1 *"Miriam and Aaron spake against Moses. It appears that jealousy of the power and influence of Moses was the real cause of their complaint; though his having married an Ethiopian woman-* האשה *הכשית haishshah haccushith = 'That Woman, the Cushite' was the ostensible cause."*

What did God have to say about all this?

"and the LORD spoke suddenly..." Numbers 12:4

Here we see God intervening in the attack. He says Moses is faithful, and upbraids Aaron and Miriam for daring to say anything against Moses. There is no word of any kind against Moses or his Ethiopian wife.

So then, who was Moses Wife?

We know that he married a girl named 'Zipporah' the daughter of Reuel/Jethro. However these people were the descendants of Abraham and Keturah (Gen.25:2). They were not the children of Ham, Cushites (i.e. Ethiopians). They were Midianites living in North West Arabia, just south of the Eastern arm of the Red Sea, known to us as the gulf of Aquaba.

Moses had fled from Egypt to this area. Midian was safe & sovereign territory that the Egyptians dared not enter. It therefore seems we must look for another wife!

Who was this Cushite and where did she come from? We are told plainly she was an Ethiopian!

First we need to identify Ethiopia.

Today this would encompass Sudan, Ethiopia and Eritrea. In a stricter sense the kingdom of Meroe from the junction of the Blue and the White Nile to the border of Egypt. "The rivers of Ethiopia" (Zeph.3:10) are the two branches of the Nile and the Astabbras (Tacazze). The City of Saba; later named Meroe by Cambyses is situated there, north of present day Khartoum. It was the Capital of the very powerful Kingdom of Meroe during the time Moses was being raised in Pharaoh's Palace, and the Ethiopians gave the Egyptians a lot of trouble as they invaded South Egypt repeatedly.

The Egyptian Victory over Meroe

Stephen, at his martyrdom, said of Moses that he was learned in all the wisdom of Egypt and mighty in words and deeds Acts 7:22. The Jewish historian Josephus tells the story of Moses in his Antiquities Chapter 10, and this was cited by Ireneus shortly after Josephus' life time:
"Josephus says that when Moses was nourished in the King's Palace, he was appointed General of the Army against the Ethiopians, and conquered them when he married that King's daughter; because out of affection for him, she delivered up the city to him."
Josephus tells us her name was 'Tharbis'. Moses won the war using a clever stratagem to take the city by surprise. He took a short cut across the narrow land between a horse shoe bend of the Nile River; clearing the snake infested ground with hungry Ibis birds, the natural enemy of snakes. So he laid siege to the city. Tharbis had seen this handsome leader of the army; fallen in love with him, and the marriage was consummated. So Moses gained a wife, he who could neither marry a Hebrew at that stage, nor an Egyptian. Moses' adoptive grandfather was Pharaoh Osirtasin I (Sesostris, Herodotus, 2:110), of the 12th dynasty, the first Egyptian king to rule Ethiopia, as a result of Moses victory.

Leaving Egypt for the Promised Land

It was customary for the daughter of the conquered King to be married into the family of the winner: if the conquered gave trouble she was basically a hostage for their good conduct. Shortly after this Moses was forced to flee Egypt, and spent the next 40 years in Midian. However when he led Israel out of Egypt it seems that he also claimed his wife of the Egyptians and took her with him. Certainly if he had left her she would have either been killed or used to pressure him to surrender.

So Moses was in reality married to two women, the Ethiopian Princess "Tharbis" and the Midianite Princess "Zipporah". While these anecdotes are not in the Bible itself, the authority for their truth is based on the historical records of the Jewish writers and Roman historians and at least one of the Church Fathers, Ireneus.

7 TWO SCARLET THREADS

The Midwife hurried across the village to the home of Judah: his daughter-in-law was now in labor, and twins were expected any moment. The startling trial five months ago had the whole village talking. Tamar had proved that Judah the son of Jacob was the father of the babies! Now the twins were about to be born, and one of them would become the Prince of the Tribe of Judah. She had brought with her a piece of Scarlet Thread to identify the first born of the two. There was a weight of responsibility attached to this birthing and she would be responsible to show which child had the rights of the First Born.

During the birthing of Tamar's twin boys, a hand first appeared, and the midwife tied a piece of scarlet thread around the wrist as he would seem to be the first born. Moments later the babies turned around in the mother's womb; and the other twin was born first. This breach meant that the one without the scarlet thread became the first born, and in that culture gained rights and privileges above the second born child.

"And it came to pass, as he drew back his hand that behold, his brother came out: and she said, 'How hast thou broken forth? This breach be upon thee:' therefore his name was called Pharez. And afterward came out his brother that had the scarlet thread upon his hand: and his name was called Zarah." Gen 38:29-30

Pharez was thus destined to be the leader of the tribe of Judah, after his father:

"Now these are the generations of Pharez: Pharez begat Hezron, And Hezron begat Ram, and Ram begat Amminadab, And Amminadab begat Nahshon, and Nahshon begat Salmon, And Salmon begat Boaz, and Boaz begat Obed, and Obed begat Jesse, and Jesse begat David." Ruth 4:18-22

Now look at Pharez' twin brother, Zarah. This was the baby that had the Scarlet Thread on his hand, but was actually born last of the two. Joshua 7:1 shows us Zerah's lineage. Zerah [Zarah] was father of Zabdi, and Zabdi of Carmi, the father of Achan. So Achan was second born, despite the scarlet thread on his wrist.

I picture Achan, just days before Passover, sitting outside his tent. He can see the forbidding walls of the city of Jericho glinting in the moonlight. The embers of his camp fire burn low as Achan thinks over 'what-could-have-been' and to his mind should have been.

Salmon, his second cousin, now Prince of the tribe of Judah, had just returned triumphant from an intelligence gathering adventure. Salmon and Phineas had entered Jericho: Jericho's King was informed of the presence of two spies in the city. To save their lives, Rahab let them down from her window in the city wall with a scarlet thread. Salmon told Rahab to display this scarlet thread in the window of her house; and promised her protection. After dramatically escaping, he reported a city shaking in its boots, fearful of the coming battle. Once more it was Salmon who had gained the fame and respect.

Old family injustices must have come to Achan's mind; his side of the family had always been the losers. Well he was a soldier now; the coming battle would be an opportunity to gain fame and valor. He was in the prime of his life, had a wife and children. He would show them what he could do!

The next day Joshua assembled the people, and instructed them to march around the city; once each day, in silence! On the seventh day they were to repeat this, seven times and then shout and attack the city: Achan could hardly wait that long. Finally the seventh day arrived, and Achan had his sword honed to a fine edge. After the final walk around the city the trumpets were blown and every man gave a shout in unison. This would surely bring the soldiers of Jericho out to fight he thought.

For a moment nothing seemed to happen, but as the echoes of the shout began to fade, a rumbling sound was heard, and before his startled gaze, the walls of this formidable city began to crack and crumble. In a moment more the walls, lined with Jericho's army, had fallen, and there was nothing left to fight. The Israeli soldiers simply walked straight through the swirling dust, over the ruins of the walls and into the city. Achan could not take this in. No fight? No chance to rise to fame? Now what could he do?

As he tramped the streets, walking among the ruins that had been part of the city, he saw a beautiful woven garment of Babylonish design, literally, as Albert Barnes notes, "a robe or cloak of Shinar, the plain in which Babylon was situated.

It was a long scarlet robe such as was worn by kings on state occasions. "This one may have been the royal robe of the King of Jericho. The same Hebrew word for 'Babylonish garment is used in Jonah 3:6 for the robe that the King of Nineveh wore, and laid aside at Jonah's preaching. Daniel too was promised "thou shalt be clothed with scarlet, and have a chain of gold about thy neck, and shalt be the third ruler in the kingdom." For Achan this could be the royal apparel that his scarlet birth thread should have entitled him to. Perhaps that was what motivated Achan to steal it.

It half covered a quantity of gold and silver; possibly the King's treasure, now exposed among the ruins. Well if he could not fight and gain fame, he would at least become wealthy. Achan stooped, gathered up the loot and slipped out of the city. His mouth almost watered at the thought of what he could do with these riches. Soldiers were entitled to the loot of a conquered city; and he was satisfied with his gains. He buried them in his tent, as his wife and children looked on.

At that very moment, Salmon was rushing with a squad of soldiers to the one remaining piece of the city wall where Rahab and her family were waiting in her house. He conducted them safely out of the city ruins, to a place apart, near the Israeli camp. They would need to be ritually clean before being accepted into the camp. Salmon felt personally responsible for Rahab and her family; and he rather liked her looks! The only survivors out of the city of Jericho, were Rahab the prostitute and her family, who were spared by identifying themselves with a Scarlet Cord. They were preserved according to the promise of the spies, and incorporated among the Jewish people.

Rahab married Salmon, whom Jewish tradition names as one of the spies; the other spy seems to have been Phinehas, the son of the High Priest Num 25:11; Josh 22:20.

"Salmon begat Boaz of Rahab; and Boaz begat Obed of Ruth; and Obed begat Jesse; and Jesse begat David the king" Matthew 1:5-6.

So Salmon, son of Pharez the first born, had his name incorporated in the lineage of Jesus. He became famous the hero of the Intelligence mission into Jericho; whose life was saved by the Scarlet Thread.

Achan thought he had gotten away with his loot, but God was watching. God had instructed the people at Mt. Sinai that the first tenth of all their increase was His.

He ordered this first looted city be untouched by the people, and promised them they could have all the loot after that. Achan was aware of the order, but his covetous heart and his jealous nature rebelled.

His act brought the anger of God upon the entire nation! Albert Barnes explains Joshua 7:1:

"It is certain that one only, was guilty; and yet the trespass is imputed here to the whole congregation; and the whole congregation soon suffered shame and disgrace on this account, as their armies were defeated, thirty-six persons slain, and general terror spread through the whole camp. Being one body, God attributes the crime of the individual to the whole, till the trespass was discovered, and by a public act of justice inflicted on the culprit; the congregation had purged itself of the iniquity."

God directed the leaders how to find the culprit, Achan. Achan's wife and children were complicit in failing to report the theft, having seen Achan bury the stuff in the ground inside their tent; and he, with his whole family, was put to death for his direct disobedience to the command of God.

The choices we make determine our future; regardless of our past. Achan, whose grandfather, Zarah, was born with a scarlet thread on his hand, never understood that the Scarlet Thread was redemptive only for those who looked to God. Your ancestry is not as important as your attitude, for we are not saved by lineage or works, but by faith in the Savior, Jesus, who was a descendant of Salmon and Rahab in the tribe of Judah.

8 AARON'S GRANDSON

The tribes of Israel were encamped on the plain east of the Jordan River, in the scanty shade of acacia trees, waiting to cross over into the Promised Land.

Balak the King of Moab hired Balaam to curse them; but he was prevented by the Angel of the Lord. Balaam did however give King Balak a stratagem to bring grief on the Israelites, advising him to encourage the Moabite women to consort with and seduce the Israelite men, Revelation 2:14. This resulted in a deathly plague that spread among the Israeli people, killing 24,000 of them. The women were not just lower class, but even royalty, for Zimri the son of Salu, a prince of the Simeonite tribe, consorted with a Midianitish princess, Cozbi, daughter of Zur, a chief ruler, and brought her publicly into his tent in the sight of the Israeli people; mourning their dead by the plague. This was a public affront, and rebellion against the Laws of God.

Enter Aaron's Grandson!

The young man Phinehas was standing near the Tent of Meeting, amidst hundreds of crying people, when he saw the blatant challenge of Zimri, openly escorting the foreign woman into his own tent[3]. His upbringing as a son of Eleazar and grandson of Aaron the High Priest, gave him instant understanding of the enormity of the offence. Thousands were dying of a plague, and the anger of God was upon the people for their sexual immorality.

Here were Zimri and Cozbi openly challenging the standards God had set for his people. His blood boiled, he grabbed a javelin, and went into the tent after them. Phinehas in the name

---

[3] Exodus 6:25

of righteousness thrust both of them through, putting them instantly to death.

At that very moment the virulent spreading plague stopped. God spoke personally to Moses commending Phinehas and promising that this young man would one day become the High Priest and his priesthood would be enduring for perpetuity Num 25:10-12.

Shortly after this God commanded Moses to avenge the injustices perpetrated against Israel by the Midianites.

Moses then personally selected Phinehas to war against the Midianites taking with him one thousand soldiers from each of the 12 tribes of Israel. They achieved an overwhelming victory, and amazingly not one single soldier of the 12 thousand was killed. Phinehas returned from the battle as a hero in the eyes of the people of Israel. Now after the death of Aaron, Eleazar, Phinehas' father, became the High Priest in the 40th year of their exodus from Egypt Num 33:38.

Within a few short weeks Moses too, died and the mantle of leadership fell upon Joshua.

His task was to take the people of Israel across the flooding Jordan River to occupy the land promised to them by God. Five miles west of the river lay the walled city of Jericho, armed and ready to withstand a siege or attack. Joshua could not afford to bypass this city, and be attacked from the rear.

It was vital that he obtain reliable information about the strength and morale of the people of Jericho.

He deliberated on who he could trust with this sensitive secret mission. Joshua knew the calamitous result of sending men to scout the land forty years ago, only two were still alive, himself and Caleb. He now needed young trustworthy men for this job, and perhaps two would be enough.

Joshua needed men of integrity and courage as well as standing with the people.

He immediately thought of Salmon, the young Prince of Judah. As he considered his options he remembered how Salmon's cousin, Phinehas had distinguished himself in the matter of Zimri, and how God had approved the young man's actions. One day he would become the High Priest after his father passed on, but right now he seemed best qualified for the work in hand.

Joshua summoned the two young men, Salmon and Phinehas, to a meeting and tasked them with the job of penetrating the enemy lines and gathering the needed information. Both of them knew that they might never return alive from this dangerous intelligence mission.

Just crossing the river was a challenge.

The moon was waxing nightly and the Jordan was in the spring flood stage, almost a mile wide, having risen beyond its banks. How they accomplished this we are not told, but the made it and sauntered into Jericho in the late afternoon. There was one place where information could be obtained, and that was the local inn, where people gathered to talk and eat. There they met with Rahab, who risked her life, telling them all they needed to know, misleading the king's messengers, and then making a covenant with Salmon and Phinehas, to protect her father, mother and family.

Phinehas also pronounced 'Pincas' according to the writings of the Jewish Rabbins has an interesting family connection.

His father Eleazar married the sister of Nashon, the prince of Judah[4]. Nashon's son Salmon, the prince of the tribe of Judah, was therefore his cousin, and one of the two spies that entered Jericho accompanied by his cousin Phinehas.

Rabbi Avraham ben Yaakov postulated Caleb of Judah, as the other spy[5], but Joshua 6:23 says they were 'young men that were spies'.

Caleb was in his 80's but Salmon was a young man and the context shows he had made covenant with Rahab. In my chapter, "Two Scarlet Threads I have traced the line of Salmon who married Rahab the woman who protected them in Jericho.

Phinehas went on to become the high priest after his father Eleazar's death and remained in office for 19 years.

His descent is traced in scripture all the way down to Ezra who went into captivity in Babylon. According to Septuagint Phinehas was buried with his father in Ephraim on the hill Gibeah Joshua 24:33. The tomb of Phinehas is shown at Awertah, four miles S.E. of Nablus, in the center of the village, within an area overshadowed by an old vine, according to Fausset's Bible dictionary. His character was marked with strong moral indignation and fine integrity.

---

[4] www.sacred-texts.com/chr/bb/bb33.htm
[5] www.azamra.org/Bible/Joshua%202.htm

9 CALEB - ONE IN A MILLION

Did you know that nearly 3 million people left Egypt to go to the Promised Land of Israel? Of those that left Egypt only 2 actually entered the Land of Eretz Israel!

Early in their exodus, the Israelites sent 12 spies into the Promised Land to assess the potential. The spies returned with a majority report that was negative. God was angry with the lack of faith of the men and sent a plague on them. Ten died, only 2 were spared. Who were they? The two who brought the Minority report of Faith, saying we can conquer the land with God's help. These were the same two who entered the Promised Land. They were Joshua and Caleb. Caleb was really 'One in a Million'.

Who was Caleb and what did he accomplish that made a difference in history?

First we are told he was a Prince in Israel, a family chief of the tribe of Judah Num 13:2, 6. Caleb has a name with meaning to it, as many people did in that time. Many carelessly take the name to mean "dog" but the International Standard Bible Encyclopedia has this interesting comment: *"kā'leb (כלב, kālēbh; in the light of the cognate Syriac and Arabic words, the meaning is not "dog," which is כלב, kelebh, in Hebrew, but "raging with canine madness"; Χαλέβ, Chaléb)"* So he is characterized as an 'Attack Dog', we would call that a K-9 Police Dog today! Trained and fearless; ready to do what it took, to win in a conflict!

After the return from the reconnaissance expedition, no mention of Caleb appears during the span of 45 years until Caleb petitions Joshua at Gilgal after 5 years of conquest in the Promised Land; and its division amongst the tribes. Now he reminds Joshua of the Promise of God to give Caleb the land his feet trod upon Joshua 14:6-14.

The old man is now 85 years of age, but the 'Police Dog' is not done yet!

He prepares to attack the city. He proceeds to take the city and drive out the three sons of Anak the Giant Joshua 14:14.

He immediately moves against another stronghold, Kirjath-sepher (Debir). The fierce opposition encountered leads Caleb to offer in marriage his beautiful and influential daughter, Achsah as a reward to the General who takes the city Jos 15:16. Caleb's nephew Othniel takes the challenge and wins the hand of Achsah. With the Bride came an inheritance of good South facing land, ideal for agriculture, and at the instance of his daughter's request, he granted exclusive water rights, a valuable commodity in that culture Jos 15:18-19. We learn that the City of Hebron was given to the Levites, the ministering priests, but the land and fields around it were given to Caleb Jos 21:12.

What is the significance of this?

In this territory lay the field and cave of Machpelah. This was a double cave by meaning of the word 'Machpelah', bought from Ephron the Hittite by Abraham, the ancestor of Caleb. Here Sarai, or as most know her Sarah, was buried and later; here Isaac and Ismael buried Abraham. Caleb knew what he wanted when he went to conquer Hebron; formerly called Kirjath-Arba, the city of the Giants. He drove the giants out of his territory, killing many of them. A few escaped to the territory of the Philistines on the Mediterranean coast and four brothers of them later became a terror to Israel until David killed Goliath and David's men finally killed the other three.

Caleb, the first real Giant-Slayer stands out as a fearless fighter, tough in his old age, not thinking of settling into retirement, he married Ephratah and their son Salma founded Bethlehem, the city of David where Jesus was born 1 Chron 2:50-51.

The reason that Caleb was singled out was repeatedly stated to be that "He fully followed Jehovah" Num 32:12.

The man had real trust and faith in God. He was tough; a soldier, a man of vision and a Patriot. He believed that God had sent Abraham to the Promised Land: and 400 years later used him, Caleb, to fulfill the promise God made that the descendants of Abraham would inherit the land.

"And these all, having obtained a good report through faith, did not receive the promise, for God had provided some better thing for us, that they should not be made perfect without us." Heb 11:39-40

What an inspiration to you today, to walk in faith with a soft heart and a strong belief in the promises of God.

10 THE GOOD OR THE BEST?

The tribes of Israel were poised to enter the Promised Land by crossing the Jordan River.

A deputation came to make a deal with Moses and the Leadership of Israel. These were the leaders of the tribes of Reuben and Gad, joined by half the tribe of Manasseh. They were enamored with the looks of the land from the middle point east of the Dead Sea, bordering the East Bank of the Jordan River, all the way up to the very northern tip of the Sea of Galilee.

These tribes had large herds of cattle and saw this territory as being the very best grazing land. Their eyes were upon what they saw as being so much to their own benefit that they were willing to even forego immediate possession. They first conquered the area; they settled their wives and children in fortified towns and then left them there while they accompanied the rest of the Army of Israel to conquer the land of Canaan. Having fulfilled their contract with Moses and Joshua and the leaders of Israel they returned to live on the East Bank territory of what had formerly been the land of Jazer and Gilead and Bashan Numbers 32:1-5.

During the assignment of the 12 tribes at Sinai, we find Gad united to Reuben on the south side of the Tabernacle. Companionship in arms and hardships in the wilderness naturally led them to desire neighborhood in their possessions; also similarity of pursuits in tending flocks and herds led Gad to an alliance with Reuben. Like Abraham and Jacob, they two alone of the tribes remained shepherds still; after the intervening centuries since Jacob left Canaan for Egypt. They therefore received the pasture lands east of Jordan for their possession; best suited for their "multitude of cattle," but accompanied the nine and a half tribes across Jordan to war with the Canaanites.

Only after their conquest and the apportionment of the whole land to their brethren "at the doorway of the tabernacle of the congregation in Shiloh, before Jehovah" Joshua.19:51; 22:1-8, were they dismissed to their tents for they still led a half nomadic life) in the land of their possession. This decision by the Reubenites and Gadites was based on their lust to have what they saw as most advantageous to themselves. The early history of Reuben seems to have repeated itself again here. His dying father, Jacob tells him;

"Reuben, you are my firstborn, my might and the beginning of my strength, the excellency of dignity and the excellency of power. Unstable as water, you shall not excel, because you went up to your father's bed; then you defiled it-" (Genesis 49:3-4).

Here we learn of his foul incest with Bilhah his father's secondary wife, and his loss of the right of the First Born as punishment.

I have heard it said that 'what you focus on you come to desire for yourself.' In the case of Reuben and Gad they wanted what God had not planned for them. Was there no suitable pasture land on the west of the Jordan? They did not know, but they grabbed what looked good to them, perhaps on the "I want it now" philosophy. Certainly it was not in the perfect will of God.

They paid the price for their choice.

Having remained on the East of the Jordan, they were vulnerable to attack by marauding bands, as they soon found out, and finally found themselves in the path of the cruel King of Assyria.

"In the days of Pekah king of Israel, Tiglath-Pileser king of Assyria came and took Ijon, Abel Beth Maachah, Janoah, Kedesh, Hazor, Gilead, and Galilee, all the land of Naphtali; and he carried them captive to Assyria."2 Kings 15:29

In 740 B.C. Tiglath-Pileser III, King of the Great Assyrian Empire, whose capital was a complex of four cities, the composite later named Nineveh, carried away the Reubenites, the Gadites, and half of Manasseh, placing them as captive slaves in cities of Assyria. God's plan was to use pagan Nineveh's example to teach the covenant people Israel how inexcusable is their impenitence. Just one generation earlier Jonah preached to Nineveh and they repented. 140 years later these same people exact a judgment on Reuben and Gad. The mills of God grind slowly, but exceeding fine! Hope to the penitent, however sunken; condemnation to the impenitent; however elevated in privileges. These are the lessons our Lord draws from Nineveh Matt. 12:41.

Sadly the Reubenites and Gadites reaped trouble and captivity instead of the blessing that God had intended for them. They chose Earthly blessing instead of the Spiritual. Is this just some old history lesson?

Is it not true that our modern world is doing the same thing? I as an individual have many times faced the temptation to grab the good instead of God's best.

If you have been making 'good' choices instead of 'God's best' this might be a good time to turn your heart toward the Lord; who longs to give you better than you or I deserve.

11 PEOPLE OF THE "LITTLE TOWN"

One small town was mentioned a few times in the Bible, and then two thirds of the way through the book, it is never mentioned again!

Situated five miles South of Jerusalem; it is 2,350 ft. above sea level. It occupies an outstanding position upon a spur running East from the watershed with deep valleys to the Northeast and South It is just off the main road to Hebron and the south, but upon the highroad to Tekoa and En-gedi. Just a small town, but peopled by men and women who made history. History records stories of some amazing people who came from this small town. Let me tell you about a few of these heroes.

The first one I find is a man named Salma.

You may never have noticed him but he had a famous father, Caleb, one of only two men who survived the 40 years in the Wilderness and was allowed to enter the Promised Land. At that time Caleb at age 80 years conquered the mountainous region of land just west of the Salt Sea. His son Salma found a beautiful area that was perfect for farming wheat and began to farm the area and the little town that developed was called 'Fruitful', in Hebrew Ephrath, later Ephraim. These were the days of conquest and a man had to be strong to build and defend his territory.

In close proximity to Ephraim there stood a 400 year old Tomb. Here was buried the wife of one of Salma's ancestors, Rachel. She died giving birth to her son Benoni; as she named him with her dying breath. His father Jacob however called him Benjamin. The Benjaminites were almost exterminated in a feudal war with the other tribes of Israel, and remained a very small tribe.

Now who are these, coming so dejectedly out of the town gate of Ephraim with their few possessions on their shoulders? They are Elimelech; his wife Naomi; with their two young sons, Mahlon and Chileon.

The drought had struck again as it did every few years, and in desperation they were leaving to find some way to survive in the country of Moab. They settled down there for some years, and the boys grew and took them each a wife of the Moabites.

Sadly Elimelech and both the sons died, and left the wife and mother destitute.

Wondering what to do, Naomi overheard a traveler say that the rains had come to the land of Judah, and the crops were growing again. She decided that she would return to her home town and take the charity of the law that allowed the poor to pick up the remnants of the crop left by the harvesters. When they finally reached Ephrath, the people exclaimed "Is this Naomi?" The name meant "Lovable" but she said, "Call me Mara, for God has dealt bitterly with me." Her daughter in law Ruth elected to go with her and would not be dissuaded. God directed Ruth to glean wheat in the field of Boaz, who later married her. Little did Naomi know that she would be the grandmother to Obed, whose son Jesse fathered a shepherd boy, David, who became King of Israel.

Some years later we meet a man named Elkanah

He was an Ephrathite who moved his residence to Ramah, and as a Levite he took his family to worship at the Tabernacle each year. His barren wife, Hannah was severely provoked by his second wife, and went to pray for a child at the Tabernacle. The priest accused Hannah of drunkenness; such was her anguish, as she wordlessly prayed for a son. When the priest understood her problem, he prophesied she would have a son. She responded with the vow that if she had a son she would give him to God as long as he lives. The son of this Ephrathite and was born to her and they named him, Samuel. So, God gave to the nation a Prophet whose fame was greater perhaps than any other in Israel. The time came when the Lord sent Samuel to this 'Little Town' of Ephrath, to find a King among the 8 sons of Jesse, and he anointed the youngest, a shepherd boy to be King of Israel.

We know him as King David, the warrior King who killed the giant Goliath

When the Philistines captured his home town and made it their stronghold; David voiced his longing for a drink of the cool water from the well on the edge of the town. So great was his leadership, that two of his mightiest men broke through at the risk of their lives to bring him that drink of that water for which he thirsted.

When King David had ruled for many years his son, Absalom, sought to usurp the Kingdom, and David fled to find sanctuary east of the Jordan. Finally his son was killed, he returned to Jerusalem. Now Barzillai was a very aged man, eighty years old. He had provided the king with supplies while he stayed at

Mahanaim; for he was very rich. David invited Barzillai to accompany him back to Jerusalem and to live off the King's bounty. He declined the offer but suggested his son might go with David.

"But here is your servant Chimham; let him cross over with my lord the king, and do for him what seems good to you". David agreed, and Chimham went with David.

Fausset's Bible Dictionary reports: *"In Jeremiah's time the caravansary of Chimham near Bethlehem was the usual starting place for Egypt.* Jeremiah 41:17. The inn mentioned in Luke 2 was a similar one, and possibly the same" 2 Samuel 19:37-40. At the return of the Jews from Babylon, Only one hundred and twenty-three "children of Bethlehem" accompanied Zerubbabel Ezra 2:21; Nehemiah 7:26.

After this a cloak of silence falls over this obscure little village, for more than 400 years.

One night some Shepherds are told by Angels that in this little town of Ephrath, the promised Messiah has been born. They find and worship the Baby in a Manger in this little town. About four months later a group of foreigners camp by the well. They are Astronomers, belonging to the Babylonian elite, known as Magi. They have been following a star, and now at midnight they stand around the well to see if indeed the star is exactly on the meridian.

The ancients did not have telescopes, but by gazing down a deep well, they could see when a Star was exactly overhead by its reflection in the water at the bottom of the well. It was; and they entered the town at sunrise to seek the Baby born King of the Jews. They brought Him gifts and worshipped Him.

Within a week, blood flowed in the streets of Bethlehem-Ephrath.

King Herod the Great hearing of the birth of the new King ordered the murder of every child under the age of 2 years. The voices of bereaved mothers could be heard crying for their children from a long way off. This was the little town of the Prophet Micah's famous prophecy Micah 5:2.

"And you, Bethlehem Ephratah, you being least among the thousands of Judah, out of you He shall come forth to Me, to become Ruler in Israel, He whose goings forth have been from of old, from the days of eternity."

There is an old Church marking the place where the baby was born. He grew to manhood, went willingly to die on a Cross to pay for your sins and make a way for you to find Peace with God, by accepting His gift of complete forgiveness. May you find Him for yourself; as wise men did so long ago. The Bible seems to forget about Bethlehem after this, but tells us to the last page, all about the One who was born there. His Name is Jesus Christ.

12 BENAIAH SON OF JEHOIADA

What kind of a man would enter a slippery snowy pit with a lion trapped in there? Benaiah did! Let's look at what we know about this man and then I will give you my best guess as to why he did that.

This man Benaiah was a man of extraordinary courage.

He is mentioned as going down into a pit on a snowy day, and killing a lion that was trapped therein 1 Chronicles 11:22. He is also renowned for his victory over two Moabite Heroes, described as 'lion-like men and for killing an Egyptian giant, while he had only a staff for a weapon, by grabbing his opponents spear and killing him with it.

He was more famous than the listed 30 mighty men, of King David's followers. His extraordinary courage and absolute commitment to his leader was known to all, and David appointed him as head of his personal body guard 1 Chronicles 11:24-25.

His family roots.

His father was Jehoiada, a Prince leader of the Aaronic line of 3,700 Priests who joined David at Hebron at the commencement of his reign 1 Chronicles 27:5. Here was a man grown up in a godly home, conversant with the Scriptures and the worship of God. Benaiah was of the priestly line, the son of a Priest, yet a warrior and strong leader, becoming prominent in the leadership; who served David to the end of his reign 1Kings 1:32.

His loyalty to David is implied in the decision of David's son Adonijah, not to invite him to join in the conspiracy to overthrow David 1Kings 1:10.

From the scripture references it is clear that Benaiah served David for all 40 years of David's reign and then at least a couple more under Solomon.

He was a married man, and had at least two sons, Jehoiada, who succeeded Ahitophel as David's chief councilor and who was named after his grandfather 1 Chronicles 27:34, and Ammizabad a warrior who is not mentioned again in scripture 1 Chronicles 27:6.

He was appointed to secure the crowning of Solomon.

When the conspiracy of Adonijah was made known to David, and confirmed by Nathan the Prophet, David summoned Benaiah into his presence and ordered him and Nathan with Zadok the Priest to put Solomon on a mule and go to the fountain of Gihon, just outside Jerusalem's south western wall, near the King's Palace. He ordered the entire bodyguard under Benaiah to accompany them, probably for security, and then we find Benaiah heartily agreeing with the King's command, saying,

"Amen! May the LORD God of my lord the king say so too. As the LORD has been with my lord the king, even so may He be with Solomon, and make his throne greater than the throne of my lord King David" 1 Kings 1:36-7.

There was good reason for this action as Adonijah and his followers were barely a 1/4 mile south of the fountain of Gihon, at Enrogal Josh 18:16. Jonathon, son of Abiathar the priest, ran to warn Adonijah and his followers of what had happened and actually quoted Benaiah's prayer! King David in his last days commands Solomon to act with wisdom regarding these men who had betrayed his trust 1 Kings 2:5-9.

There are some interesting sidelights to Benaiah.

Solomon was forced to take action against his half-brother Adonijah, Abiathar, Joab and Shimei. Except for Abiathar, who was removed from his priestly duty and banished to his home in Anathoth, Benaiah was ordered to execute the others. 1 Kings 2:13-46 is the sad story of these wicked men's demise at the hand of Benaiah.

Joab fled to the Tabernacle and was holding the horns of the altar. This was the act of one who is asking for mercy, but Solomon ordered Benaiah to strike him down, as undeserving of any further grace. Benaiah arrives at the Tabernacle and, with his own Priestly background, hesitates to kill Joab in the holy place. He calls him to come out of there on the authority of the King. Joab refuses, saying 'No, but I will die here', Then Benaiah returns to the King first for further orders. Only after the King said to take Joab at his word, does this godly warrior execute Joab in the Tabernacle area. Even in his later years we find in Benaiah a sensitivity to the things of God and righteousness that is seldom found in an old tough soldier.

Historically this seems to be the end of the story of Benaiah.

Perhaps the foregoing throws some light on the introduction of this great man, who went down into a snowy pit and killed a lion. It seems to me that this was perhaps not an act of immature bravado, but an act of kindness: for if that lion was injured he would have been in pain, and needed to be put down. Certainly few men would have ventured to enter that slippery snowy pit; but just shrugged it off and left the lion to suffer and die. This man had fine principles of right and wrong and he held to them all his life.

13 A MAN KING DAVID FEARED

The Bible records the great deeds of David the Shepherd boy who became King of Israel. He killed the giant Goliath, and engaged in many battles. The Women came out of the towns singing,

"King Saul has slain his thousands and David his ten-thousands!"

We tend to picture a young boy facing a giant: but read how Saul was head and shoulders taller than the entire nation; and then suggested David wear his armor. I believe David was close to Saul in stature, or the story would have been out of context with the facts. David only objected on the grounds that he had not used such armor in battle, not that it did not fit him. So we have a fearless warrior who once crowned King made this statement.

"I am the chosen king, but Joab and Abishai have more power than I do. So God will have to pay them back for the evil thing they did." 2 Sam 3:39 CEV.

Who was Joab, and what was this power he had over David? Let's look first at his relationship, then his rapaciousness and lastly his ruin.

Relationship

Joab was one of three brothers. His brothers were Abishai who was the oldest, and Asahel the youngest. Their mother was Zeruiah the sister of David (1 Chron. 2:16). So they were David's nephews, family, and sons of his sister. When David was forced to run for his life from King Saul, he found a stronghold, where he could hide. Abishai is mentioned in connection with David's flight from Saul. David found a safe place for his parents lest Saul attack them (1 Sam 22:3-4). The first time Joab's name appears in the Bible is in 1 Sam 26:6 where David is talking to Abishai who is here called Joab's brother. The next mention of Joab is just after David has moved to Hebron.

Abner the commander of Saul's army got into a battle with David's men under Joab's leadership. This was a time of war between the tribes under Saul's son, Ish-bosheth and the followers of David (2 Sam 2:10-23). Abner was compelled to kill Joab's youngest brother Asahel to save his own life. A truce was called and it seemed that all was settled. We find the three brothers in leadership positions in David's army, mentioned among his mighty men, and finally Joab takes the city of Jebus (Later named Jerusalem) and becomes David's Army Commander 1 Chronicles 11:6.

Rapaciousness

Joab was an extremely strong and ambitious person. Abishai was the oldest, and extremely loyal to David. Asahel is mentioned number six in the list of the 'mighty men' of David 2 Sam 23:24.

Joab heard that David had made a treaty with Abner shortly after the Battle when Asahel died. He immediately saw a chance to get even with Abner. Unsuspectingly Abner returned to Hebron; only to be assassinated by Joab at the City gate 2 Sam 3:30. David was unable to punish Joab for this act.

Joab had claimed that this was a blood-feud, but David saw it as murder, for Asahel was killed in war and Joab murdered Abner in a time of peace. Joab's motivation seems to have been his fear that he would be replaced as Commander of the Army by Abner, in return for bringing the rest to the tribes of Israel under David's rule. If Abner had been really slain in revenge for blood, as Joab asserted, he ought to have been delivered up "bound hand and foot." But Joab, instead of waiting for Abner to be delivered up, with the legal formalities, to the authorized penalty as an assassin, stabbed him as a worthless fellow 1Kings 2:5.

Joab was such a vicious opponent that the Edomite leader, Hadad, took refuge in Egypt until he knew Joab was dead 1 Kings 11:21-22. Joab's murder of Amasa was equally treacherous 2 Sam 17:25. Joab continued to gain power over David, leading the Army into battle and conquering peoples around them. The Biblical account records him killing thousands of people he had captured. The final opportunity to attain power fell to Joab, when David, having sinned in the matter of Uriah's wife Bathsheba, sent a message to Joab to withdraw from Uriah in the heat of battle, so that he would be killed.

Joab now had a hold on David as partner with him in the murder of Uriah. Joab was still looking to gain more power and began to scheme to restore Absalom, to his father David. He saw that if Absalom became King after David, Joab would have a grateful new leader and one less likely to punish him than the other son of David, Solomon.

While Joab was for many years loyal to David, he finally sided with David's other son, Adonijah in his rebellion. This time there was no victory for Joab.

Ruin

When David was on his death-bed, he was informed that Joab had fled to the sanctuary of the Tabernacle, at Gibeon, near Jerusalem. There he clung to the horns of the altar of burnt offerings, hoping for mercy. This however afforded no protection for the scripture clearly states that

"If a man willfully attacks another to kill him by cunning, you shall take him from my altar that he may die." Exodus 21:14.

He was dragged from the altar and killed by Benaiah on David's orders. David then uttered a curse upon the family of Joab. Second Samuel 3:29 speaks of the descendants of Joab in terms of never having health or wealth or long life. How sad the end of a mighty man, who allowed his passions and pride to dominate his life.

It is not how well you start out but how well you finish this life's race that really counts.

"Now these things happened to them as an example, but they were written down for our instruction, on whom the end of the ages has come." 1 Corinthians 10:11.

14 ABINADAB AND ARK OF GOD

The History of the Ark of God
God commanded Moses to make a box, or Ark, to house the Tables of the Law, and to be a seat for the Lord God. This Ark of the Covenant was captured by the Philistines around the 29th year of King Saul's reign. The Ark was in the Philistines' possession for 7 months (1Sa 6:1). In consequence of the plagues that came on each city where the Ark was kept in Philistia it was reluctantly returned by them to Israel. Arrived in Beth-shemesh, it was unloaded by Levites (1 Sam 6:15); and sacrifices were offered before it that day. After opening it and looking inside; the Beth-shemeshites incurred upon themselves the curse of God, in which 50,070 men were slaughtered (1 Sam 6:19). The people of Beth-shemesh therefore declined to open their homes to it. They sent to the people of Kirjath-jearim, who were slaves and serviced the House of God with water and wood, to come and fetch the Ark 1 Samuel 6:21.

The House of the Ark of God

"And the men of Kirjath-jearim came, and fetched up the ark of the LORD, and brought it into the house of Abinadab in the hill, and sanctified Eleazar his son to keep the ark of the LORD." 1 Samuel 7:1.

We here encounter the first mention of the house of Abinadab on the hill. The Ark remained in the house of Abinadab for 20 years 1 Samuel 7:2. The village of Kirjath-jearim was grouped with Gibeah, Gibeon, and Ramah near Jerusalem Joshua 18:25-28 as they were all very close together; less than a day's walk. The area became the property of the tribe of Benjamin, and Gibeah; the home city of Kish and his son Saul.

"And Ner fathered Kish. And Kish fathered Saul. And Saul fathered Jonathan, and Malchishua, and Abinadab, and Eshbaal".

The house of Abinadab, a son of King Saul, was in Gibeah, the city on the peak of the hill" 2 Sam 6:3 where the name Gibeah is also translated, 'the hill'.

It would appear that these villages were so close to each other that they were called the cities of Gibeon, or the 'Hill Cities' 1 Chronicles 9:39.

Thirteen years after the Ark was placed in the house of Abinadab, King Saul was slain by the Philistines in a battle on Mt. Gilboa bordering the valley of Armageddon. Abinadab was also killed in that battle together with his father Saul 1Sa 31:2. This ended the 40 year reign of Saul.

David succeeded Saul as King, and reigned in Hebron 7 years. He conquered Jerusalem, made it his new Capital City, and decided to bring the Ark to Jerusalem 2 Samuel 5:3-7. Abinadab at this time is no longer alive, but the Ark is still in the "House of Abinadab" 2 Samuel 6:3.

The Honor of the Ark of God

"And they cause the ark of God to ride on a new cart, and lift it up from the house of Abinadab, which is in the height, and Uzzah and Ahio, sons of Abinadab are leading the new cart;" (2 Sam 6:3 YLT).

Dramatic tragedy erupts as the procession moves toward Jerusalem. Uzzah sees the cart lurch, stretches out his hand to steady the Ark, to keep it from falling. Fire from heaven flames out and strikes him dead 2 Samuel 6:6-8. The original Hebrew word is violent and graphic. It says that Uzzah literally exploded!

This raises questions in the mind of a reader.

The answers are to be found within the pages of the Bible.

Why were the sons of Abinadab allowed to take care of the Ark, and be involved in its transportation to Jerusalem?

Kish is listed among the Levites 2 Chronicles 29:12. The sons of Kish married the daughters of Eleazar the Priest (1 Chronicles 23:22). There were no sons of Eleazar, so the sons of Kish were Levites, the natural guardians of the Ark of God Numbers 36:8-9.

Why did God strike Uzzah dead for trying to protect the Ark of the Covenant from falling off the cart?

"And when Aaron and his sons have made an end of covering the sanctuary, and all the vessels of the sanctuary, as the camp is to set forward; after that, the sons of Kohath shall come to bear it: but they shall not touch any holy thing, lest they die" Numbers 4:14.

Uzzah was a Levite and the old saying still remains true, 'Ignorance of the law is no excuse.' The Ark of God was so sacred that God decreed that not even the Levites may touch it. It was to be honored, and revered as the Throne of God, for here was where the Glory of God descended.

David and Israel followed the Philistine method of making a new cart and attaching Oxen to it 1 Samuel 6:7, ff. David's excitement changed to self-recrimination as he realized that God was not going to accept men's ways of doing religion. It took King David three months to find out what the proper procedure was, and once they followed that, the Ark was safely brought to its place near the Holy City.

If there is one thing we can learn from this story, it is that refusing to follow the directions God laid down, does not make God go away. God makes the rules, and we are blessed when we follow them.

"Provoke me not and I will do you no hurt" says God. *(Jer 25:6).*

15 MICHAL- THE PROUD PRINCESS

W e see a young girl growing up in a family that was suddenly catapulted to Kingship. She was the youngest daughter of Saul Ben-Kish, and his wife Ahinoam. Her three brothers and her older sister Merab grew up in a home where their father was looked up to by all the community as a powerful and handsome man 1 Samuel 9:1-2 14:49-50.

Her father, Saul, had to fight for his Kingship, securing it through successful warfare. His family was not counted for much before he became King 1Sam.14:47. Usually a King's lineage was noted at the beginning of his reign, but in Saul's case it is only mentioned much later.

It would appear that Pride was however not lacking in Saul:

So Samuel said, *"When you were little in your own eyes, were you not head of the tribes of Israel? And did not the LORD anoint you king over Israel? Then he said, "I have sinned; yet honor me now, please, before the elders of my people and before Israel, and return with me, that I may worship the LORD your God." 1Samuel 15:17, 30.*

This background is important, for we see a young girl growing up in a family that was suddenly catapulted to Kingship, and she becomes very conscious of her position as the King's daughter. When David appears she hears of, if not sees, his victory over Goliath. David is promised as wife to her older sister Merab, but Merab is already promised to be the wife of Adriel the Meholathite 1Sam 18:19.

"Now Michal, Saul's daughter, loved David. And they told Saul, and the thing pleased him" 1Sam 18:20.

So the younger sister has fallen for the champion David. Saul is ready to use her as the bait to destroy David. The prospective bridegroom accomplishes Saul's life-endangering demand for a dowry and they are married. Saul is frustrated; and plots to kill David, now Michal's husband.

She warns David, helps him escape; and placates her angry father. Saul, gives her to Paltiel 1Sa 14:50, as wife.

Several years pass and David is hunted as an outlaw

On David's ascension to the throne after Saul's death, Abner offers to bring the northern kingdom of Israel into David's hands. He is told that no deal will be considered until he arranges to return Michal back to David 2 Sam 3:15. Michal is restored to David, who now already has two more wives, Ahinoam the Jezreelitess and Abigail the widow of Nabal.

For seven years after this Michal is the reigning first wife of the King

She is proud of her position in the Court of King David, and all is well until David captures Jerusalem and sets up his Palace there and brings the Ark of God's covenant into the city. When David arrives with thousands of the leaders of the tribes of Israel with the Ark, she looks out of the window and sees her husband dancing and singing in front of the Ark. This takes a long time as they stopped every few yards to offer sacrifices to God 2 Sam 6:13. Her father had not taken his religion seriously, but David her husband, has a passion for God that she does not understand. He is totally in love with his God. The Bible records her inmost emotions.

She despised him in her heart 2Sa 6:16.

She was so upset with David's *un-kingly* conduct that she could not wait to upbraid him, and she did it publicly: "she came out to meet David". Her accusations were embellished; the result of her heart's condition, 'for out of the heart the man speaketh'. David defends himself explaining that he did his worship to the Lord. He makes the point that God had set her father and his family aside and chosen him, and he was not afraid to be undignified, but would be humble in his own sight. Nowhere does David show anger or judgment to his wife, but the scripture tells us that God judged her.

"Therefore Michal, the daughter of Saul, had no children to the day of her death" 2 Sam 6:23.

If there is one thing that a woman usually wishes for, it is to have children. She was the King's first wife, and in the culture of that society, barrenness is considered a curse. Her relationship to David appears strained from this time on, but her sister Merab had five sons, and she got to raise them, and so allow her motherly instincts free reign. We do not know what happened to Merab, most commentators think she died, but in any event, Michal became in the place of a mother to them. She was deprived of this too, when the sins of her father came home to roost 2 Sam 21:2. Saul had tried to wipe out the Gibeonites, a remnant of the Amorites, with whom the children of Israel had sworn a peace treaty.

Now the Gibeonites demanded restitution in blood, and demanded the death of seven of Saul's descendants. David handed over Merab's five sons and the two sons of Rizpah, whom the men of Gibeah then hanged, 2 Sam 21:8).

The life of Michal was one of being handed over from one man to another

She was not given any choice of her own. She displayed courage in the face of great odds, risking her own life for the man she loved, and standing up to the King, her father, and to King David her husband. Sadly she seems to have had little respect for the things of God, but one can hardly help but admire her strength of character and have some sympathy for the trials she endured.

We all have things happen in our lives we cannot control; but if we leave God out of the equation we will miss the best that life has for us. Life can come at us with hard times and difficult situations, but if we honor God, he will turn things around for us. Sadly the record is that she was judged by God. 2 Samuel 6:23 says:

"Therefore Michal the daughter of Saul had no children to the day of her death".

You can gain a lot of the good things in life and overcome many obstacles, but you will find emptiness and disappointment without the blessing of God on your life. Seek Him and your life will turn around for the better.

16 AHITOPHEL COMMITTED SUICIDE!

T he Bible mentions this man in three places only, yet his life is intertwined with King David from the time that he was crowned in Hebron to the time of the death of Absalom. We are told that the counsel of Ahitophel:

"Was as if a man had inquired at the oracle of God: so was all the counsel of Ahitophel both with David and with Absalom." 2 Samuel 16:23.

Where did this man Ahitophel come from?

The Bible says he was from the town of Giloh, a town near Hebron Joshua 15:51-55. The towns of Maon, Ziph, and Carmel are all mentioned here; and are the inheritance of Caleb. He was a descendant in Caleb's line and lived close to Ziph and Carmel. This was the area where Saul hunted David, again and again, and David must perforce have made many contacts with the locals thereabouts.

When David sent his young men to Nabal, asking for something in return for having protected Nabal's shepherds and flocks from marauders in the area of Carmel he was rebuffed; and it was Abigail who saved the lives of all of them by her quick thinking and action. After Nabal died, David married Abigail. Now in 1 Samuel 25:25 you will see that she admits to the meaning of her husband's name, Nabal, which in our language means a "Fool". This is the only man in the Bible who is actually named such.

These places were all close to one another, and the feast that Nabal held, vs. 36 'like the feast of a King', was very likely attended by people from Ziph and would have known these were David's young men who came to see Nabal. Nabal is a descendant of Caleb through the line of Ziph, and the inhabitants of the city of Ziph were informants to Saul as to the whereabouts of David cf. Josephus 6, 13.

What was Ahitophel's position in the Kings court?

He was renowned for his wisdom, and understanding. We find him mentioned as the King's counselor in 1 Chron. 27:33. Just when he was appointed counselor is not clear, but from the preceding scripture it would appear that he was the first and held his position up until the time of Absalom's rebellion.

It is interesting to note that there are two probable connections to David's Court.

First the meaning of Ahitophel's name is "Brother of a Fool" If he was indeed brother to Nabal, which is probable as both were descended from Caleb, through Ziph, and lived nearby one another; and his name points that way; then Abigail may well have introduced him to her new husband David, for he would have been her brother in law and was known as a 'wise man'.

The second interesting connection is that Eliam was one of David's 30 mighty men and was the son of Ahitophel 2 Sam 23:34 also called Ammiel 1 Chron. 3:5. This brings us to the next question.

Why did Ahitophel commit suicide?

Ahitophel had faithfully served David, was close to him for years, yet suddenly he turns on his King, and joins the conspiracy of Absalom, and then Absalom dies, and finding his advice not followed he hangs himself. Herein lies an interesting tale.

You see Ahitophel was the one person who was in the know, when David committed adultery with Bathsheba. He was in the Palace, in the confidence of the King, and he was Bathsheba's Grandfather! Yes look up 2 Sam.11:3. Bathsheba was the daughter of Eliam whose father was Ahitophel.

Here is the seed of betrayal

Years later this became Ahitophel's motivation to turn on David and join Absalom. Bathsheba had been happily married to Uriah, whose name means, 'Light of Jehovah" a proselyte to Judaism and also a commander in David's army. He had been passionately in love with Bathsheba, 2 Sam. 12:3, and never knew of his wife's seduction and dishonor. David had brazenly seduced Bathsheba and had Uriah killed in battle on purpose. Ahitophel carried that grudge for years, and David never knew it. In Psalm 41:9 David laments

"Yea mine own familiar friend in whom I trusted, which did eat of my bread, hath lifted up his heel against me."

Interestingly, Jesus quoted this verse in speaking of Judas at the last supper, as the betrayer, who like Ahitophel turned against the one who entrusted him with responsibility. See also Psalm 55:12-14.

When Ahitophel's advice to Absalom, to attack David immediately and kill him was rejected, he knew that David would come out the victor and there was no future for him, so he went home, related the events to his family; and according to Josephus, he went into an inner room, hanged himself, and the family buried him.

Here was a man of wise counsel, who let bitterness enter his soul

He made an unforgivable error of judgment, in the hopes of getting vengeance on David for the seduction of Bathsheba; and the killing of Uriah. Sadly he never lived to see his great grandson, Solomon take the throne. Think about Ahitophel when you have a grudge and want to get even, and ask the Lord to take the root of bitterness out of your heart, for it will ruin you and contaminate those around you.

Hebrews 12:14–15 says, that we are to:

"Follow peace with all men, and holiness, without which no man shall see the Lord: Looking diligently lest any man fail of the grace of God; lest any root of bitterness springing up trouble you, and thereby many be defiled;"

Friend, if you have a grudge; go and make peace with the one you are at odds with. Forgiveness is a verb, not a feeling. It is something you have to do, not something you will feel, or pray for. Peace comes after you have gone to and forgiven the one you were in conflict with. Whether they accept it, or not, once you have forgiven, you will get the peace of God in your soul.

17 THE WOMEN OF SHUNEM

The first of these two women was Abishag the Shunammite During King David's last days she was selected from among the most beautiful women in the land, and brought to keep the aging King David warm. After his death she is coveted by Solomon's older half-brother Adonijah in an attempt to wrest the kingdom from Solomon, so you could say Adonijah lost his head over a woman, for he was executed for his pains.

Now it is evident that Abishag is a celebrity, and we find her who was yet a virgin, betrothed to King Solomon. She is one of the personages, celebrated in the poem of Solomon's Song 6:13

"Return, return, O Shulamite; return, return, that we may look upon thee. What will ye see in the Shulamite? As it were the company of two armies."

The name, Shulamite, denotes a woman belonging to a place called Shulem, which is probably the same as Shunem. If then Shulamite and Shunammite are equivalent, we may conjecture that the Shunammite, who was the object of Solomon's passion, was Abishag, the most lovely girl of her day, and at the time of David's death, the most prominent person in Jerusalem."

1 Kings 1:13 says that Abishag was from Shunem. This town lies on the road from Mt. Carmel to Samaria and is mentioned by Eusebius as five miles south of Mount Tabor, and then known as Sulem. This agrees with the position of the present *Solam*, a village three miles north of Jezreel, and five from Gilboa.

The town lay on the border between Israel and Canaan, in the tribe of Issachar. There appears no indication that the Israelites expelled the Canaanites from there. Certainly history holds that the most beautiful girl in the land was Abishag the Shunammite.

Did she return to her home town in her later years? Many people in those days did so, in order to be buried in the family sepulcher at their death.

Now we meet the second woman of Shunem

Fast forward your clock, 100 years, and walk the dusty road that passes by Shunem. This is the road used by the Prophet Elisha who frequently traveled this road and is recognized and known by the inhabitants of Shunem 2 Kings 4:8 ff. He had recently returned from a war fought by King Jehoram of Israel against Moab.

When Elisha first meets this second woman of Shunem, she is a noted person in the community, a great woman. Her husband has a prosperous estate, and is an old man. They have no heir, she is childless. She is presented as discreet, and compassionate. She encourages the Prophet to make their home a stopping place for rest and refreshment on his journeys. He prophesies the future birth of a son to her and her husband, which took place about a year later. What was it that people knew about her that facilitated such a reputation? It may just be speculation on my part, but I wonder, was she perhaps a granddaughter or descendent of Abishag? The girl Abishag was dark skinned, likely a Canaanite, and if she is Abishag's descendent, it may account for the fact that all communications between this woman and Elisha were carried out through Gehazi who could speak her language, while Elisha could not.

After the Seven-year drought, the Shunammite woman with her son returned from the land of the Philistines, and petitioned the King for the return of her property in Shunem (2 Kings 8:1-6).

It was a God appointed timing, as she comes into the King's presence; Gehazi is relating the story of Elisha raising this woman's son from the dead. He sees and recognizes the woman and her son; and introduces her to the King. The King ordered all her property be returned to her; including all the income from the land during the years of her absence.

When you are walking in faith, you too will experience God appointed timings in your life as did this lady.

God certainly intends you to know that He cares for you who put your trust in Him; whether you are of the stock of Israel or of the Gentiles who by faith believe the promises of God even as Abraham did.

18 RECHABITES - HAVE A DRINK, FRIEND!

oes God tell His Prophet to tempt men to violate their conscience? Here is a Prophet inviting men sworn to abstain from wine to drink some! There are three interesting truths found here.

A Separated People

The Bible refers to a family of men called Rechabites. Rechab, father of Jehonadab, belonged to the Kenites, and were connected with Israel through Moses' marriage; thus Heber and Jael, with Israel entered Canaan, and shared their inheritance, though remaining nomads in tents. The ascetic rule against wine, houses, sowing, and planting (Jeremiah 35), was a safeguard against the corrupting license of the Phoenician cities and their idolatries.

Their father was Jehonadab. He is mentioned as meeting Jehu, and was invited to go with him to witness the retribution of God on Baal (2 Ki 10:15 -28). As a man of God, his presence gave sanction to the Judgment of God as executed by Jehu.

Jeremiah the Prophet is told to invite the Rechabites to come to the Temple to meet with him Jeremiah 35:1-19. He takes them into a special room called the chamber of the sons of Hanan the son of Igdaliah, a holy man of God. As consecrated by its association with his name, it was a fit scene for the divine communication.

Their strict Nazarite vow was the ground of their admission into one of the temple chambers devoted to the sons of Hanan sprung from "Igdaliah" a man of God, or prophet of special sanctity.

A Tempted People

"Then I set before the sons of the house of the Rechabites bowls full of wine, and cups; and I said to them, 'Drink wine.'" Jer 35:5

They were invited by the Holy Prophet of God, Jeremiah to partake of wine in a consecrated room, in the very Temple of God. It is very easy to find people who will look at circumstances around them and say to themselves, 'It must be alright to do this in this situation, even though we would never do it elsewhere!' The Rechabites had taken a vow to obey the commands of their forefather and no matter the setting or circumstances; they remained true to their commitment. There is a common feeling today that times alter the standards by which we should live.

The fallacy is preposterous. The law of Gravity is still the same, because it is the product of the Creator of the Universe. He has given us warnings in His Word, the Bible, to keep us from harm. His Truth does not change because of time, or circumstance. If we obey His advice, we will be on solid ground, and when we take our commitment to Christ seriously, we need to see that there are certain non-negotiable standards of separation from what others view as permissible. Like the Rechabites we may be tested by God, to see if we will remain true to what we profess.

A Remembered People

"And Jeremiah said to the house of the Rechabites, 'Thus says the LORD of hosts, the God of Israel: 'Because you have obeyed the commandment of Jonadab your father, and kept all his precepts and done according to all that he commanded you, therefore thus says the LORD of hosts, the God of Israel: Jonadab the son of Rechab shall not lack a man to stand before Me forever.' Jer 35:18-19.

This prophecy was fulfilled: After the return from captivity in Babylon the Rechabites are mentioned 1 Chronicles 2:55 as taking the profession of Scribes, an occupation almost exclusively that of the Levites. A tradition exists that the Rechabites married Levites, and their children ministered in the temple. Eusebius quotes Hegesippus as mentioning a Rechabite priest protesting the martyrdom in the temple, of James the Just, half-brother of Jesus. So Hegesippus reveals the existence of the Rechabites as being involved in the temple right up to the time of its destruction by the Romans. This fulfills the prophecy of Jeremiah 35:19.

Benjamin of Tudela, who lived in the 12th Century speaks of 100,000 Rechabites living in Pumbeditha, Babylonia, a major center of Talmud scholarship in the late 3rd century, abstaining from wine and meat and says that their Chief, Solomon han Nasi, was a descendent of David.

As I look at the Rechabites, I am encouraged to know that when we live up to the standards of the Bible, and God's Word, we too may be remembered by Him, who died on the Cross to pay for our past sin and gives us new life, and says we are in this world system, but not of it.

The same word for Test, Tempt and Trial is used in the Bible. How are we to distinguish between these? Just remember that "God Tests us", "I go through trials" and "The Devil Tempts us to do wrong". I encourage you to take a stand for right living, and recognize that the standards our forefathers held to were worthwhile, and for our good. Remember the Rechabites!

19 GEHAZI – THE TESTING OF A PROPHET

After Elijah was taken to heaven, Elisha found a man who he would mentor as he had been mentored. On the surface all looked well; he faithfully served and did Elisha's bidding. He translated the Prophets words to a Gentile Shunammite woman who had often given them lodging as they traveled past her home. She was barren, and Elisha prophesied she would have a son, which happened as he said. A few years later the child died, apparently of an aneurism to the brain. She laid the child on the bed used by Elisha and traveled to find the Prophet.

The First Test

When Elisha heard what happened, the bible tells us what he did.

"Then he said to Gehazi, Gird up thy loins, and take my staff in thine hand, and go thy way: if thou meet any man, salute him not; and if any salute thee, answer him not again: and lay my staff upon the face of the child" 2 Kings 4:29.

Gehazi was given Elisha's staff: in that culture a sign of authority; and commissioned to go straight to the dead boy and revive him.

"And Gehazi passed on before them, and laid the staff upon the face of the child; but there was neither voice, nor hearing. Wherefore he went again to meet him, and told him, saying, 'The child is not awaked'. And when Elisha was come into the house, behold, the child was dead, and laid upon his bed" 2 Kings 4:31-32.

Here is a Prophet in Training, but even with the Prophetic Commission and the Staff, he was powerless! Did Elisha have more power than other prophets? The short answer is–No! None of the men of God had any power. The signs and wonders are done by God's power. So the problem was not the power but the person. There has to be a spiritual flow from the Lord through those He uses to perform His mighty acts. This leads me to look for signs of intrinsic flaws in the character of the man Gehazi.

The Second Test

This brings us to the next event in which Gehazi is specifically named. The Army Commander of the Syrian King, was a leper, and finds his way to Elisha seeking healing. Miraculously healed he offers to give Elisha money and clothing. Elisha refused the proffered gifts, told Naaman to go in peace. The bible picks up the story with the interesting word 'but'.

"But Gehazi, the servant of Elisha the man of God, said, Behold, my master hath spared Naaman this Syrian, in not receiving at his hands that which he brought: but, as the LORD liveth, I will run after him, and take somewhat of him" 2 Kings 5:20.

He was not about to let some money and rich clothing from Damascus get away from him.

The Judgment of God.

His return to the presence of Elisha resulted in a showdown. Elisha knew by the Spirit of God what foreign kings were planning, and yet Gehazi thought the Prophet would not know what he was up to!

"But he went in, and stood before his master. And Elisha said unto him, 'Whence comest thou, Gehazi?' And he said, 'Thy servant went no whither'. And he said unto him, 'Went not mine heart with thee, when the man turned again from his chariot to meet thee? Is it a time to receive money, and to receive garments, and olive yards, and vineyards, and sheep, and oxen, and menservants, and maidservants?'" 2 Kings 5:25-26.

Justly, Elisha sentences Gehazi to the very sickness that Naaman had just been cured from. He became a leper and the prophet said his children would likewise be lepers, which was not necessarily a judgment, but the normal effect of an infectious disease, for which there was no treatment in those days.

What happened to Gehazi?

Our story places Elisha as living in Samaria at this time. Gehazi loses his job and as a leper is living outside the city with his sons. Now a short while later in 2 Kings 7:1 the city is under siege and famine is in their midst, but verse 3 tells us that there were four leprous men sitting outside the city gate. Despairing of their lives they decide to surrender to the Syrians, but find God has done a miracle and the Syrian Army is fleeing for their lives.

"And when these lepers came to the uttermost part of the camp, they went into one tent, and did eat and drink, and carried thence silver, and gold, and raiment, and went and hid it; and came again, and entered into another tent, and carried thence also, and went and hid it." 2 Kings 7:8 The Jewish Rabbinical writings state that these were Gehazi and his sons.

If true; their actions accurately reflect Gehazi's previous conduct. Later we find him in conversation with the King of Israel.

"And the king talked with Gehazi the servant of the man of God, saying, Tell me, I pray thee, all the great things that Elisha hath done"
2 Kings 8:4.

So Gehazi was still around to tell about the things God had done through Elisha, but not through himself. When God works through a man, he chooses one who walks before Him with a pure heart, and honest motives. When our hearts are right we will seek God's Presence and not the Perks! Perhaps if we spent more time seeking to live pure lives; we would see more manifestations of God's power in our lives. Jesus said:

"Blessed are the pure in heart; for they shall see God" Matt 5:8.

20 THE CREDITOR HAS COME

*N*ow there cried a certain woman of the wives of the sons of the
prophets unto Elisha, saying, Thy servant my husband is dead; and
thou knowest that thy servant did fear the LORD: and the creditor
is come to take unto him my two sons to be bondmen. And Elisha said unto
her, What shall I do for thee? tell me, what hast thou in the house? And she
said, Thine handmaid hath not anything in the house, save a pot of oil." 2
Kings 4:1-2

The Widow's Appeal

She appealed to Elisha, the Leader of the school of the
prophets. Adam Clarke notes that this should read: " נבייא תלמידי -
talmidey nebiyaiya, 'disciples of the prophets:' so the Targum here,
and in all other places where the words occur, and properly too."

She reminded Elisha of the faith and fervor of her late
husband. According to the Chaldee, Jarchi[6], the Rabbins, and the
historian Josephus this woman was the wife of Obadiah. As
administrator of King Ahab's Palace; He had hidden 100 prophets
in two caves; and fed them for a protracted length of time during
the period of Jezebel's introduction of Baal Worship in Israel. The
Targum says that Obadiah had borrowed money from Ahab to
feed these prophets, because he could not support them from
Ahab's estate. Elijah spared Obadiah's life; when sent to summon
Elijah to meet with Ahab.

She related the consequences of bankruptcy in this
particular instance. The creditor wanted to take her sons as slaves.
As slaves, they provided tangible commercial value, which would
be subtracted from the debt she owed. The creditor was entitled to
hold them and use their labor for up to six years.

---

[6] Jarchi http://words.fromoldbooks.org/Chalmers-Biography/ij/jarchi-
solomon-ben-isaac.html,

"If thou buy a Hebrew servant, six years he shall serve: and in the seventh he shall go out free for nothing." Exodus 21:2.

The Widow's Resources

She had two sons, whose labor was regarded as a valuable resource. She owned a small flask of anointing oil. The King James Version Bible states that she had a 'pot of oil,' which in Hebrew means *a small flask of oil.* אָסוּך from סוּך, an anointing flask - a small vessel for oil necessary for anointing the body. She had nothing else, no furniture, pots or containers. Seemingly, everything had been liquidated. However, there remained an outstanding balance owed to her creditor.

The Widow's Deliverance

When she approached the Prophet, Elisha himself had no money or resources apart from the power of God upon his life. He asked her what she had. Her response was a small horn of oil used to anoint the body. Elisha knew that oil had commercial value. He then instructed her to begin pouring it out as an act of faith. Her obedience to the instruction of the man of God resulted in the miracle of multiplication. The only limitation to her deliverance was the limited number of containers, which she borrowed from her neighbors. The oil, which she collected, was sufficient to repay the balance of her husband's debt and still have enough remaining capital to meet the needs of her and her family.

Each Hebrew family owned a permanent inheritance of land. With the help of her sons, she would be able to farm the land and purchase a few sheep or goats, to serve as the foundation of a new flock; and provide a comfortable living for her family.

When Obadiah used a line of credit to honor the God of Israel by protecting and feeding His prophets, the Lord made sure that she would be adequately taken care of. It came in the form of His Divine Provision. The widow of Obadiah literally took it to the bank! There are times when you too will need to trust God for the supernatural. God is still in the miracle business.

The Widow's Cruel Creditor

Her husband, Obadiah had borrowed the money from his boss, King Ahab. Now Ahab had died and his widow finds she is saddled with the debt.

This, says Jarchi, was Jehoram son of Ahab, who had a legal right of redress. While Elisha was more of a diplomat than Elijah was, his relations with Jehoram ran hot and cold. He was almost rude to Jehoram during the campaign against the Moabites.

However, he was willing to perform a miracle for the widow of Obadiah even if ultimately King Jehoram would benefit by it.

While the Bible clearly says the 'borrower is the slave of the lender' there are times when credit can be used with discretion. Let your lifestyle honor God by living within your means.

I believe that the words I recently read on a Church marquee are worth reflection. It said, "Act Your Wage!

21 QUEEN ATHALIAH OF JERUSALEM

Our story begins with a godly King who set his heart to seek the God of Abraham, Isaac and Jacob. His name was Jehoshaphat. 2 Chronicles 17:3 says:

"Now the LORD was with Jehoshaphat, because he walked in the former ways of his father David; he did not seek the Baals."

Unfortunately, he made a fundamental mistake.

"Jehoshaphat had riches and honor in abundance; and by marriage he allied himself with Ahab." 2 Chronicles 18:1.

Ahab was King of the Northern Ten Tribes of Israel, and it was common practice to make alliances with other nations in the lands of the Bible. You will discover as you continue reading the story that this marriage alliance was the result of his son, Jehoram, marrying the daughter of King Ahab. Now Jehoshaphat's eldest son, Jehoram, was appointed the new King in Jerusalem when his father died. At this point, the Bible records a very interesting statement about the state of affairs

"And he walked in the way of the kings of Israel, just as the house of Ahab had done, for he had the daughter of Ahab as a wife; and he did evil in the sight of the LORD." 2 Chronicles 21:6.

Whoever you marry, will affect your future here: and perhaps forever.

What, you may ask, was the evil he did?

Verse four reveals the chilling tale of Jehoram killing all six of his brothers with the sword as well as many other princes of Israel. He then proceeded to impose his wicked authority over the people in addition.

In the sixth year of his reign, Elijah the Prophet wrote him a letter. He warned Jehoshaphat of the judgment of God that was coming. He said, you will *'become very sick with a disease of your intestines, until your intestines come out by reason of the sickness'* which occurred over the following 2 years, resulting in his demise.

At age 32 he died, as the story so tragically records, 'to no one's sorrow'. This left Athaliah, the Queen Mother and her only remaining son, Ahaziah, to rule the Kingdom.

"Then the inhabitants of Jerusalem made Ahaziah, his youngest son, king in his place, for the raiders who came with the Arabians into the camp had killed all the older sons. So Ahaziah the son of Jehoram, king of Judah, reigned. Ahaziah was forty-two years old when he became king, and he reigned one year in Jerusalem. His mother's name was Athaliah the granddaughter of Omri. He also walked in the ways of the house of Ahab, for his mother advised him to do wickedly." 2 Chronicles 22:1-3

Ahaziah foolishly joined his Uncle, Jehoram, King of Israel, in a fight against Jehu and was killed. Notice the comment in the previous passage; his mother walked in the ways of her father Ahab and advised her son to do wrong!

"Now when Athaliah the mother of Ahaziah saw that her son was dead, she arose and destroyed all the royal heirs of the house of Judah." 2 Chronicles 22:10

This strong willed woman seized control of the Kingdom of Judah and killed all her grandchildren! She was determined to hold complete domination as regent Queen Mother. No one was going to grow up and usurp her reign. Six long years passed and it seemed that she was in full control.

Where was the Almighty God in all this?

When evil rulers are in charge, the people groan under the burdens and oppression. It sometimes seems as if this old world is an unjust place. What was the thing that changed the story? There is one word in the narrative that changed everything. It occurs at the very beginning of the six-year reign of Athaliah, "BUT. . . "

"But Jehoshabeath, the daughter of the king, took Joash the son of Ahaziah, and stole him away from among the king's sons who were being murdered, and put him and his nurse in a bedroom. So Jehoshabeath, the daughter of King Jehoram, the wife of Jehoiada the priest (for she was the sister of Ahaziah), hid him from Athaliah so that she did not kill him. And he was hidden with them in the house of God for six years, while Athaliah reigned over the land." 2 Chronicles 22:11-12

King Ahaziah had a sister, Jehoshabeath, who married Jehoiada, the High Priest of the Temple in Jerusalem. Jehoshabeath managed to smuggle one little baby, Prince Joash, out of the palace, and hid him in the Temple.

Six years was about all the people could stand of this wicked Queen's rule.

Jehoiada the high priest, arranged for the crowning of this now seven-year-old child, to supplant his grandmother.

"And they brought out the king's son, put the crown on him, gave him the Testimony, and made him king. Then Jehoiada and his sons anointed him, and said, "Long live the king!"

Now when Athaliah heard the noise of the people running and praising the king, she came to the people in the temple of the LORD.

When she looked, there was the king standing by his pillar at the entrance; and the leaders and the trumpeters were by the king. All the people of the land were rejoicing and blowing trumpets, also the singers with musical instruments, and those who led in praise.

So Athaliah tore her clothes and said, "Treason! Treason!" And Jehoiada the priest brought out the captains of hundreds who were set over the army, and said to them, "Take her outside under guard, and slay with the sword whoever follows her." For the priest had said, "Do not kill her in the house of the LORD." So they seized her; and she went by way of the entrance of the Horse Gate into the king's house, and they killed her there."

This was the horrible end to the life of the only Queen to rule in Jerusalem. The question that arises is: "How could a woman be so unprincipled; cruel; and corrupt?"

She had her own grandchildren murdered in cold blood and would stop at nothing to retain her hold of the throne. She also forced the worship of Baal upon the Jewish nation. As Dr. Peterson's version of the Bible translates 2 Kings 23, it was a religion which organized the worship of the 'obscene phallic Asherah Poles; set up rooms for male sacred prostitutes in the Temple of God, as well as sex-and-religion shrines across the nation'.

Well, as commentator Paul Harvey would say, here is the rest of the story!

Many years before all this happened, Athaliah's grandfather Ethbaal became the High Priest of Baal in Sidon. He then murdered Phelles the King of Sidon, and became both King and High Priest of the Phoenician's religion. His daughter married King Ahab and forced Baal worship on the Northern Kingdom of Israel. Ahab then gave her daughter Athaliah in marriage to Jehoram the King of Judah.

This was the religion of Athaliah

Athaliah grew up under the overpowering influence of her mother, and was dedicated to the religion of Baal: a god who demanded worshippers sacrifice their babies to him. This was done by creating a huge metal hollow image with outstretched hands, as a sort of tray. This Baal image was heated from below by fire until it glowed red-hot. The worshippers would then drop their baby into the waiting 'hands' of the idol, which would then open to allow the screaming burning infant to drop alive into the fire below Jeremiah 19:5.

Did I omit to tell you her mother's name?

Athaliah's mother was none other than Jezebel! When rulers forget the God of our fathers; that nation will come under judgment, unless the people return to the faith that totally trusts in our Creator God and His son, the Lord Jesus Christ, and no other.

He paid for the sins of all of us on the Cross of Calvary, that we might have peace with God and eternal life hereafter.
"Righteousness exalts a nation, but sin is a reproach to any people."
Proverbs 14:34.

22 HANAMEEL'S FIELD IN ANATHOTH

When Solomon the son of David ascended to the throne, there were some 'loose ends' that needed to be taken care of. He did so promptly, meting out justice that had been in abeyance until David's death. He took action against his elder brother who was again scheming to usurp the throne, and then banished Abiathar the Priest to his home village. This was at one time a prosperous town, from whence came some well-known biblical people.

In 1 Kings 2:26 we read: *"And unto Abiathar the priest said the king; Get thee to Anathoth, unto thine own fields;"*

This is a little village almost 3 miles northeast of Jerusalem, with some 50 inhabitants today. Once it was an important city with suburbs, and fields around it. In the days of the settlement of the land under the leadership of Joshua, it was designated as the property of the Levites, and a City of Refuge for any person accused of homicide.

Anathoth lies on a ridge of the Judean hills, with nothing to shelter it from the blistering desert winds from the east. There is a wonderful view to the southeast over towards the Jordan River and the Dead Sea, with the mountains of Moab visible in the distance. Nearby are stone quarries that still supply stones to Jerusalem for building repairs. Around the few houses are the remains of ancient walls and foundations, denoting the former greatness of this place. In close proximity to Anathoth there remain to this day, Olive and Fig trees, and fields of grain still producing harvests, a legacy of the Priests who first settled here.

Two of King David's mighty men were from Anathoth

We read of Abiezer, one of the 'Thirty', and Jehu, a warrior of renown; but he was not the Jehu of Samaria. 2 Samuel 23:27; 1 Chronicles 12:3

Ahimelech and his family were from Anathoth

The High priest at the time of King Saul's reign, he was executed together with 84 other priests for unknowingly giving aid to David as he fled from Saul. He left behind him an only son, Abiathar, who escaped with the vestments of the High Priest, and found refuge with David.

Abiathar was installed as the High Priest after the death of King Saul

He was loyal to King David for many years, until Zadok was appointed Co-High Priest with him. Then he sided with David's son Adonijah in an attempt to usurp the throne. Shortly after David's death, Solomon banished Abiathar to Anathoth for his part in the conspiracy. (1 Kings 2:26) His ancestral fields became his only source of income.

Abiathar was a descendant of Eli in the line of Ithamar a son of Aaron, whose conduct brought a prophecy of doom upon his priestly line to fulfillment. When Abiathar sided with Adonijah against Solomon, his own actions sadly brought the prophecy to fulfillment. From that time on Zadok, of the line of Eleazar reclaimed the office of High Priest. (1 Samuel 2:27, 30-31, 1 Kings 2:35)

It was in Anathoth that the 'Weeping Prophet' Jeremiah was born

His father was a godly priest, Hilkiah. Here Jeremiah heard the voice of God as a young man;

"Before I formed thee in the belly I knew thee, and before thou camest forth out of the womb I sanctified thee; I have appointed thee a prophet unto the nations." Jeremiah 1:4

Jeremiah was held captive in Jerusalem for prophesying that the King of Babylon would sack the city. The people became fearful of the future. For a few weeks the Babylonians unexpectedly withdrew from Jerusalem to deal with an attack from Egypt (Jeremiah 37:5).

Hanameel was born in Anathoth

Jeremiahs cousin, Hanameel, came to Jerusalem during this lull, to sell his field in Anathoth to Jeremiah. Having had foreknowledge and direction of the matter; by divine revelation (Jer 32:6-7); Jeremiah signed the deed of purchase and paid over the money.

This was designed by God to be a prophecy that the time would come when once again the people would return to the land after the exile, and regain their historic possessions.

"And I bought the field of Hanameel my uncle's son, that was in Anathoth, and weighed him the money, even seventeen shekels of silver"- Jeremiah 32:9

Jeremiah prophesied up to the time of the fall of Jerusalem under the Babylonian siege, and was threatened with death by his fellow townsmen of Anathoth. He was fearful for his life, but God promised that the people of Anathoth would be punished by the sword and famine, which came to pass exactly as predicted in Jeremiah 11:21-23.

The few Anathothites, who survived the siege of Jerusalem, were taken to Babylon and only 128 returned to Anathoth a generation later.

The more you study the fulfilled prophecies of the Bible the more you understand that God holds the future in His hands, and protects His own as He did Jeremiah of Anathoth.

23 AHASUERUS THE LION KINGS

*A*nd in the reign of Ahasuerus, in the beginning of his reign, wrote *they an accusation against the inhabitants of Judah and Jerusalem."* Ezra 4:6

One of the challenges to the Bible is for the reader to identify the difference between a person and a title. Many times a title is used in referring to a person, and his actual name is not noted. There can be some confusion in understanding when the title is used, while the events referred to span more than 100 years in time.

Here in the book of Ezra we have a reference to Ahasuerus, but this name is a title, and there is actually more than one person who carried that title in the Bible, and in history. The purpose of this article is to clear up the confusion and help you understand the meaning and origin of the title and look at the people who were called by that name.

I will first deal with the title: its meaning and usage. Then I will list the recipients of the title and discuss the events and times to which the Bible links these individuals.

Ahasuerus

According to the International Bible Encyclopedia, *"the name in the Persepolitan arrow-headed inscriptions is Kshershe. Xerxes is explained by Herodotus as meaning "martial"; the modern title "Shah" comes from ksahya, "a king," which forms the latter part of the name; the former part is akin to shir, a lion. The Semitic Ahashverosh equates to the Persian Khshayarsha, a common title of many Medo-Persian kings."*

Those of you who are old enough will remember the leader of modern day Persia, now called Iran, was the Shah, a king. The reputation of these rulers was implicit in the title, Lion Kings. They were known for their cruelty to those they conquered and those who lived in perpetual slavery under them.

Recipients of the Title

I find three persons who carried that title:

First of these in chronological order is Cyaxares, (B.C. 634) the son of Astyges' daughter, and Cambyses, first king of Persia.

The second is Cambyses, Cyrus' son. (B.C. 529) named after his grandfather.

The third is Xerxes, (B.C. 485), the son of Darius Hystaspes.

Look at the dates approximating the beginning of each one's reign. There are 95 years from Cyrus to Cambyses, and 44 years to Xerxes. Our attention however is drawn to the three Ahasuerus or Lion Kings because their lives impacted the people of God's Covenant, Israel. So let us look at these three in order of their appearance on the stage of world history.

Ahasuerus 1

The first of the Lion Kings was Cyaxares (B.C. 634).

The Graecized form is *Cyaxares*; the first king of Media. He gathered an army, and with the assistance of the Babylonians mounted attacks on northern Assyria. Now if you have read the book of Jonah in the Bible, you may remember that God sent Jonah to Nineveh, to preach repentance to these people and their king. This was in the time of the reign of Jeroboam II and Joash, so this was within the time frame of B.C. 823 - 780. The King and the nation repented, and God spared them. By the year B.C. 612 about 185 years had passed when Nineveh was finally destroyed. That equates to several generations. This was the King who finally fulfilled the prophecy of Jonah, after the nation of Assyria turned away to their earlier practices.

The prophet Nahum predicted the destruction of Nineveh in the book that bears his name. The following items were to be a part of the destruction of that great city: An "overflowing flood" would "make an utter end of its place" (Nah. 1:8) Nineveh would be destroyed while her inhabitants were "drunken like drunkards" (Nah. 1:10) Nineveh would be unprotected because "fire shall devour the bars of your gates"

The downfall of Nineveh would come with remarkable ease, like figs falling when the tree is shaken (Nah. 3:12-13) Nineveh would never recover, for their "injury has no healing" (Nah. 3:19).

A famous oracle had been given that "Nineveh should never be taken until the river became its enemy." After a three month siege, "rain fell in such abundance that the waters of the Tigris inundated part of the city and overturned one of its walls for a distance of twenty stades. Then the King, convinced that the oracle was accomplished and despairing of any means of escape, to avoid falling alive into the enemy's hands constructed in his palace an immense funeral pyre, placed on it his gold and silver and his royal robes, and then, shutting himself up with his wives and eunuchs in a chamber formed in the midst of the pile, disappeared in the flames. Nineveh opened its gates to the besiegers, but this tardy submission did not save the proud city. It was pillaged and burned, and then razed to the ground so completely as to evidence the implacable hatred enkindled in the minds of subject nations by the fierce and cruel Assyrian government." (Lenormant and E. Chevallier, '*The Rise and Fall of Assyria*').

Ahasuerus II

The second of the Lion Kings was Ahasuerus II - Cambyses (B.C. 529). This was the Ahasuerus of Ezra 4:6. The enemies of the Jews tried to stop the building of the temple by sending a letter of accusation to Cambyses, Ahasuerus II. He took no action on the matter, probably knowing the true facts of the case; he viewed it as an invalid accusation. He however only reigned for 7 ½ years.

Ahasuerus III

Our third and final Lion King was Ahasuerus III - Xerxes (B.C. 485-465). I found an interesting quotation in Fausset's Bible Dictionary concerning this Xerxes:

"*Xerxes in his third year held an assembly to prepare for invading Greece. In his seventh year Ahasuerus replaced Vashti by marrying Esther (Est. 2:16), after gathering all the fair young virgins to Shushan: so Xerxes in his seventh year, on his defeat and return from Greece, consoled himself with the pleasures of the harem, and offered a reward for the inventor of a new pleasure (Herodotus 9:108). The "tribute" which he "laid upon the land and upon the isles of the sea" (Est.10:1) was probably to replenish his treasury, exhausted by the Grecian expedition."*

This was the king who allowed the decree to destroy the entire Jewish people at the suggestion of Haman the Agagite; and then to prevent this irrevocable decree, permitted the Jews to kill thousands of his subjects in self-defense.

A cruel king; his history is documented by Herodotus, and he really earned the title of 'Lion King'.

Around the world today we are witnessing the arrogance of 'Lion Kings' of this ilk, but there is a passage that the followers of Jesus can hold dear. It is found in Psalm 2:9-11 "*Thou shalt break them with a rod of iron; Thou shalt dash them in pieces like a potter's vessel. Now therefore be wise, O ye kings: Be instructed, ye judges of the earth. Serve Jehovah with fear, and rejoice with trembling.*"

Study the Bible, and look up, for your day of redemption is close at hand.

24 HISTORY AND VISIONS

My Purpose here is to present to you two similar accounts, one a factual historical record, the other a man's account of a Vision he said he had. Weigh up the two accounts, compare them and ask yourself; were they talking about the same things? If so which was written first? First here is the Historical account of the events with the dates of the saga. Then I will relate the story written by the man who says he had a vision. So here they are and if they appear to be the same then you decide which was written first, the History or the Vision?

History of the Conquest of the Persians by Alexander the Great

The true hero of the story of Alexander is not so much Alexander as it is his father *King Philip of Macedonia*. The author of a piece does not shine in the limelight as the actor does, and it was Philip who planned much of the greatness that his son achieved, who laid the foundations and forged the tools, who had indeed already begun the Persian expedition at the time of his death. Philip, beyond doubt, was one of the greatest monarchs the world has ever seen; he was a man of the utmost intelligence and ability, and his range of ideas was vastly beyond the scope of his time. He made Aristotle his friend; he must have discussed with him those schemes for the organization of real knowledge which the philosopher was to realize later through Alexander's endowments.

Philip made this little barbaric state into a great one; he created the most efficient military organization the world had so far seen; and he had brought most of Greece into one confederacy under his leadership at the time of his death. His extraordinary quality, his power of thinking out beyond the current ideas of his time, is shown not so much in those matters as in the care with which he had his son trained to carry on the policy he had created. He is one of the few monarchs in history who cared for his successor.

Alexander was, as few other monarchs have ever been, a king specially educated for empire. Aristotle was but one of the several able tutors his father chose for him. Philip confided his policy to him, and entrusted him with commands and authority by the time he was sixteen. He commanded the cavalry at Chaeronea under his father's eye. He was nursed into power—generously and un-suspiciously.

To anyone who reads his life with care it is evident that Alexander started with an equipment of training and ideas of unprecedented value. As he got beyond the wisdom of his upbringing he began to blunder and misbehave, sometimes with a dreadful folly. The defects of his character had triumphed over his upbringing long before he died. Philip was a very great and noble man, and yet he was drunkard, who could keep no order in his household.

Alexander was in many ways gifted above any man of his time; he was also vain, suspicious, and passionate; with a mindset awry by his mother.

From the very beginning of his reign in 336 B.C. the deeds of Alexander showed how well he had assimilated his father's plans, and how great were his own abilities. After receiving assurances from Greece that he was to be captain-general of the Grecian forces, he marched through Thrace to the Danube; Thebes—unsupported of course by Athens —was taken and looted; it was treated with extravagant violence; all its buildings, except the temple and the house of the poet Pindar, were razed, and thirty thousand people sold into slavery. Greece was stunned, and Alexander was free to go on with the Persian campaign. From there he marched through Asia Minor to Persia.

King Darius the 3rd of Persia had a force of two hundred Chariots as well as his infantry. Darius began the battle by flinging them against Alexander's cavalry and light infantry. Few reached their objective and those that did were readily disposed of. There was some maneuvering for position.

The well-drilled Macedonians moved obliquely across the Persian front, keeping good order; the Persians, following this movement to the flank, opened gaps in their array. Then suddenly the disciplined Macedonian cavalry charged at one of these torn places and smote the center of the Persian host. The infantry followed close upon their charge. The center and left of the Persians crumpled up. For a while the light cavalry on the Persian right gained ground against Alexander's left, only to be cut to pieces by the cavalry from Thessaly, which by this time had become almost as good as its Macedonian model. The Persian forces ceased to resemble an army.

They dissolved into a vast multitude of fugitives streaming under great dust-clouds and without a single rally across the hot plain towards Arbela. Through the dust and the flying crowd rode the victors, slaying and slaying until darkness stayed the slaughter.

Darius led the retreat

Such was the battle of Arbela. It was fought on October the 1st, 331 B.C. We know its date so exactly because it is recorded that, eleven days before it began, the soothsayers on both sides had been greatly exercised by an eclipse of the moon. Darius fled to the north into the country of the Medes.

Alexander marched on to Babylon.

The ancient city of Hammurabi (who had reigned seventeen hundred years before) and of Nebuchadnezzar the Great and of Nabonidus was still, unlike Nineveh, a prosperous and important center. Like the Egyptians, the Babylonians were not greatly concerned at a change of rule to Macedonian from Persian. The temple of Bel-Marduk was in ruins; a quarry for building material, but the tradition of the Chaldean priests still lingered, and Alexander promised to restore the building. Thence he marched on to Susa, once the chief city of the vanished and forgotten Elamites, and now the Persian capital.

He went on to Persepolis, where, at the climax of a drunken carouse, he burnt down the great palace of the king of kings. This he afterwards declared was the revenge of Greece for the burning of Athens by Xerxes. Alexander had been in undisputed possession of the Persian Empire for six years. He was now thirty-one years of age.

This last story and many such stories may be lies or distortions or exaggerations. They do have a vein in common. After a bout of hard drinking in Babylon a sudden fever came upon Alexander 323 B.C. he sickened and died; he was only thirty-three years of age. The world empire he had snatched at, and held in his hands, as a child might snatch at and hold a precious vase; fell to the ground and was shattered to pieces. His siblings and mother were all murdered, and he left no one to take his place.

There presently emerged four leading figures from this welter of crime.

Much of the Old Persian Empire was held by one general Seleucus, who founded a dynasty, the Seleucid Dynasty; Ptolemy a Macedonian, secured Egypt. Lysimachus became the governor of Thrace, and Cassander, of Macedonia and Greece. This is the Historical and factual account of what happened as recorded by today's historians ("The Outline of History" (Book 1. H.G. Wells. Doubleday & Co. 1961)).

Now here is a Story of a man who has a vision and recounts it.

Listen for the similarities and ask yourself when you think this story was written.

"In the vision, I saw myself in Susa, the capital city of the province Elam, standing at the Ulai Canal. Looking around, I was surprised to see a ram also standing at the gate. The ram had two huge horns, one bigger than the other, but the bigger horn was the last to appear. I watched as the ram charged: first west, then north, then south. No beast could stand up to him. He did just as he pleased, strutting as if he were king of the beasts. "While I was watching this, wondering what it all meant, I saw a Billy goat with an immense horn in the middle of its forehead come up out of the west and fly across the whole country, not once touching the ground. The Billy goat approached the double-horned ram that I had earlier seen standing at the gate and, enraged, charged it viciously. I watched as, mad with rage, it charged the ram and hit it so hard that it broke off its two horns. The ram didn't stand a chance against it. The Billy goat knocked the ram to the ground and stomped all over it. Nothing could have saved the ram from the goat."Then the Billy goat swelled to an enormous size. At the height of its power its immense horn broke off and four other big horns sprouted in its place, pointing to the four points of the compass.

"While I ...was trying to make sense of what I was seeing, suddenly there was a humanlike figure standing before me." And then he said, 'I want to tell you what is going to happen. The double-horned ram you saw stands for the two kings of the Medes and Persians. The Billy goat stands for the kingdom of the Greeks. The huge horn on its forehead is the first Greek king. The four horns that sprouted after it was broken off are the four kings that come after him, but without his power.

"'But now let me tell you the truth of how things stand: Three more kings of Persia will show up, and then a fourth will become richer than all of them. When he senses that he is powerful enough as a result of his wealth, he will go to war against the entire kingdom of Greece. Then a powerful king will show up: and take over a huge territory and run things just as he pleases. But at the height of his power, with everything seemingly under control, his kingdom will split into four parts, like the four points of the compass. But his heirs won't get in on it. There will be no continuity with his kingship. Others will tear it to pieces and grab whatever they can get for themselves".

That is the Vision recorded as a story. Is this a description of the events described in Historical records?

While there is verbal imagery used in the vision account, the facts coincide in incredible detail with the previous historical account. Was this Vision story then written after the event? There are scholars who think so. Why? Because the human probability of such a vision being predicted before the event seems impossible for them to accept.

However the writer of the vision was a man, of whom King Nebuchadnezzar of Babylon said: *"The great God has let the king know what will happen in the years to come. This is an accurate telling of the dream, and the interpretation is also accurate".*

When Daniel finished speaking; King Nebuchadnezzar fell on his face in awe before Daniel. He ordered the offering of sacrifices and burning of incense in Daniel's honor. He said to Daniel:

"Your God is beyond question the God of all gods, the Master of all kings. And he solves all mysteries, I know, because you've solved this mystery."

Daniel came as a captive of Nebuchadnezzar to Babylon, and was there when Belshazzar succeeded Nebuchadnezzar 43 years later.

"In King Belshazzar's third year as king, (of Babylon) another vision came to me, Daniel".

When then did this Vision take place? It took place in the 3rd year of the Babylonian King Belshazzar 538 BC. That same night, Darius the 1st conquered Babylon and slew Belshazzar. Alexander the Great only arrived and conquered Persia in 331 B.C.

So the vision was experienced and recorded 207 years before Alexander's historical conquest.

Archeologists have found proof that this vision account is true. Babylon's capture by surprise during a festival was foretold in Jer.51:31; Jer.51:39, one hundred and seventy years earlier, and that the capture would be by the Medes and Persians in Isaiah.21:1-9.

Berosus' account of the king not being slain, and Daniel's account of his being slain: supposed once to be an insurmountable difficulty; is fully cleared up by the monuments. Rawlinson found clay cylinders in Umqeer (Ur of the Chaldee's), two of which mention Belshazzar as oldest son of Nabonahit. Berosus gives the Chaldean account, which suppresses all about Belshazzar, as being to the national dishonor.

Had the book of Daniel been the work of a late forger, he would have followed Berosus' account which was the later one. If Daniel gave a history different from that current in Babylonia, the Jews of that region would not have received it as true. Darius the Mede took the kingdom at the age of 62, upon Belshazzar's death.

Rawlinson thinks that he was set up by Cyrus, the captor of Babylon, as viceroy there, and that he is identical with the Median king Astyages, son of Ahasuerus (Cyaxares), whom Cyrus, the Persian king, deposed but treated kindly. The phrase in Daniel 9:1, "Darius, son of Ahasuerus (Cyaxares), of the seed of the Medes, which was made king over the realm of the Chaldeans," implies that Darius owed the kingdom to another, i.e. Cyrus.

This vision then can only be attributed to the Creator God who has all knowledge of the future, and who reveals secrets to his servants who listen to Him. God's knowledge written before an event is termed prophecy.

The vision Daniel had, was simply God telling us that what He reveals in His book is 100% accurate. The Bible has many such incredible stories written before the fact! There are over 300 prophecies predicting the birth of Jesus. All were exactly fulfilled.

There are many more predictions of His promised second return to earth. Many of these future prophecies mirror things we see as we watch today's news. You need to make sure your relationship with Jesus is such that He will say "I know you as one of my followers, welcome!"

25 AN INTERUPPTED CONVERSATION

Hank boarded the bus to work, each day, and would start a conversation with his friend; then stopped speaking as the bus arrived at his building. Eight hours later he boarded the bus to return home, sat down next to his friend and picked up the conversation exactly where he had left off. The intervening time did not seem to have affected him at all.

When God spoke to Israel through the last Old Testament prophet, Malachi; He said, *that he would send Elijah*; to turn the heart of the fathers to their children, and the heart of the children to their fathers. This prophecy ends abruptly.

It was followed by a resounding Divine silence; for a period of 400 years. Then God appeared to a Priest in the Temple, and picks up the conversation that was interrupted; saying to him "Fear not, Zacharias: for thy prayer is heard; and thy wife Elisabeth shall bear thee a son, and he shall go before him in *the spirit and power of Elijah*, to turn the hearts of the fathers to the children, and the disobedient to the wisdom of the just; to make ready a people prepared for the Lord (Luke 1:13, 17)."

Zacharias was an old man, and had given up hope of having a son; his wife also being barren. He obediently named him John. At the baby's dedication, Zacharias was filled with the Holy Spirit, and prophesied, "thou, child, shalt be called the prophet of the Highest: for thou shalt go before the face of the Lord to prepare his ways; to give knowledge of salvation unto his people by the remission of their sins, through the tender mercy of our God."

Within a year of John's birth, Herod the Great instituted a manhunt for the baby Jesus, whom the Magi came to seek as 'King of the Jews'. Word of the strange events surrounding the birth of John had circulated, and Herod demanded that Zacharias hand over baby John. Zacharias had foreseen this possibility and hid the child.

The soldiers of Herod reported this to the king, and were ordered to murder Zacharias in cold blood right there in the temple.

Jesus, in a scorching denunciation and prophecy to the Scribes and Pharisees; said: *"Upon you may come all the righteous blood shed upon the earth, from the blood of righteous Abel unto the blood of Zacharias son of Barachias, whom ye slew between the temple and the altar. Verily I say unto you, all these things shall come upon this generation Matt 23:35."* Within 35 years the temple was no more!

Theodosius, a Byzantine traveler, wrote in his diary in the 6th century that the Biblical Zacharias, the father of John the Baptist, was martyred and buried in a tomb just outside the eastern wall of the temple.

Legends have surrounded this tomb for centuries; it was popularly called Absalom's tomb when I saw it in 1966. That all changed in 2001 when Joe Zias, a Jerusalem archeologist from the Israeli Antiquities Authority, identified an inscription on it that read *"This is the tomb of Zacharias, martyr, a very pious priest, father of John the Baptist[7]."*

The Scribes and Pharisees, who controlled the Temple, still wished to get rid of John; so he remained in hiding until he was of age to begin his ministry. Luke closed his first chapter, writing *"And the child grew, and waxed strong in spirit, and was in the deserts till the day of his showing unto Israel."*

John's dress and habits were strikingly suggestive of Elijah, the old prophet of national judgment[4]. It is not improbable that he intentionally copied his great prophetic model Elijah. Like John you may not understand circumstances and current events. You can rest in the same answer that Jesus sent to John; prophecies were being fulfilled. Jesus identified Johanan ben Zacharias, as the one promised; and he referenced Malachi chapter three: saying "Verily I say unto you, among them that are born of women there hath not risen a greater than John the Baptist: and if ye will receive it: *"this is Elijah which was to come"* Matt 11:11."

It does not matter how many years you live; what does matter is that you seek and find the plan of God for your life; and fulfill the purposes of God for your generation!

---

[7] www.biblesearchers.com/hebrewchurch/archaeology/zachariasimeon.shtml

26 CAESAR AUGUSTUS AND JESUS BIRTH

He rose from relative obscurity to become the most powerful man in the world before he died. Born September 23, 63 BC, Octavianus, was the nephew of Julius Caesar, and was raised by his grandmother and Julius Caesar's sister, Julia Caesaris. Caesar adopted him as his son and heir. Upon his adoption he took the name of his great-uncle Gaius Julius Caesar. He later took the name Augustus, meaning 'honorable' and so great became his power and leadership that the following Caesars all took that same title on becoming his successors.

Augustus slowly acquired a succession of job titles; to consolidate his power, and hold, over the Roman Senate. At two different times in his career he took the temporary office of Consul. He served as a Consul in the years 5 and 2 BC. In this capacity he was empowered to determine the membership of the Roman Senate; and to hold a Census throughout the Roman Empire. In a document titled, 'Res Gestae Divi Augusti' – recounting his deeds as Emperor he wrote:

'A third time, with the consular imperium, and with my son Tiberius Caesar as my colleague, I performed the census in the consulship.' -2-8 Res Gastae.

The Senate bestowed on Caesar Augustus the title of 'Pater Patriae' or 'Divine Father of the Country' in 2 BC. It was the 750th Anniversary of the founding of Rome, and Augustus' 25th Anniversary since becoming Caesar. It was decreed that all the inhabitants of the Roman Empire be registered in their city of origin, and swear allegiance to him as the 'Pater Patriae'. (Lewis & Reinhold, Roman Civilization, vol. II, pps. 34-35, Harper Torchbooks Edition)

"Now it came to pass in those days, there went out a decree from Caesar Augustus, that all the world should be enrolled." Luke 2:1 ASV

St. Luke clearly writes in the Greek text that this was an enrollment, and not a tax; as the old King James Version translates the word.

Many scholars assumed that Luke had made a mistake here; but documents and inscriptions have since come to light that confirmed the Lukan assertions in every detail.

Little did the great Caesar Augustus realize that his decree would set in motion the placing of Joseph and Mary in Bethlehem, in perfect time for the prophetic fulfillment of the birth of Jesus, the son of God. In a very real way Caesar Augustus became a divinely directed participant in the first Christmas. The Bible says that: *"The king's heart is in the hand of the LORD, as the rivers of water: he turneth it whithersoever he will." Prov 21:1.*

Perhaps the Lord is working in your circumstances in a way you feel may be inconvenient. I am quite sure that Joseph and Mary must have felt that way; as they walked the 70 miles to Bethlehem.

It is important to know that God is in control of your life when good things happen; and also when things happen that you are not content with. We live in a world of uncertainty and change. It is here that we can trust God until He makes us look in the rear view mirror. Then we begin to see clearly that we were in God's plan all the time.

27 THE HORRIBLE HERODS

While many people have read of 'Herod' in the Bible; few of us are clear about who we are reading about. The truth of the matter is that the Herod of one Bible reference; may not be the same person in another; the family has an incredibly long history. While claiming to be Jewish, the Herodians were not of pure Jewish stock.

Herod Antipas I - ?-78 BC

Herod Antipas 1st was a descendant of Esau (or Edom), also known as an Idumean; who married Cypros, an Arabian Lady of noble descent. Herod Antipas 1st was appointed governor of Edom by Alexander Janneus and he held this position until his death in 78 BC.

Herod Antipater - ? - 43 BC

Herod Antipater succeeded his father in 78 BC and was given the Procurator ship of Judea by the Roman Caesar the in 47 BC. He was assassinated in 43 BC and left four sons and a daughter. The names of his children were: Phasael, Herod the Great, Joseph, Pheroras, and Salome.

Herod the Great - (Circa) 71 BC – 1 AD

This is the first Herod mentioned in the Bible. Herod was a young man of about 20 years of age, possibly as old as 25, when he assumed his career with the appointment to be governor of Galilee. Josephus states that "he continued his life to a very old age." In 41 BC Mark Antony appointed him tetrarch of Judea and in 37 BC he obtained the crown of Judea as a king under Caesar Augustus of Rome: He ruled 37 years" (Appian- Roman History).

His first marriage was to Mariannme the granddaughter of John Hyrcanus, who had been the high priest of the Jews and first leader of the Maccabee rebellion. Herod was afraid to leave any remnant of that dynasty alive at his death that might endanger his successors, so he had her executed in 28 BC together with her mother Alexandra, and just before he died, he arranged the execution of two of his sons by her, Alexander and Aristobulus a week before his own demise.

His final days were full of conspiracies and efforts by his sons to usurp his throne. He suffered an incurable loathsome disease of the bowels, which stank; debilitating him to the point of attempting suicide. The cause of death was chronic Kidney disease, complicated by Fournier's Gangrene.

It was in the last weeks of his life that he was visited by the wise men from the East seeking the newborn king of the Jews. The journey of the wise men from Susa, Persia, took about 150 days, and we know that Mary remained in Bethlehem for at least 40 days after Jesus birth to fulfill the purification rites for a first born male child. So the late 1 BC visit to Jesus by the Magi is not too far off from probability. Herod invited the wise men to come back and tell him when they had found the newborn baby; but when they did not return within the week, he issued the order for the slaughter of all the newborn children in Bethlehem of two years and under. Jesus would have been 5 months old then.

Herod died after an insurrection had occurred at the Temple entrance, a mob pulling down the offensive Golden Eagle that Herod had erected. This puts his death at the time of Passover, in the 37th year of his reign. *"The principal conclusion is that Herod died in early 1 A.D. because the December 29, 1 B.C. eclipse was the most likely to have been widely observed, and all of the historical evidence can be explained by the one simple hypothesis that Josephus was not aware that Herod's successors had antedated their reigns."* (johnpratt.com/items/docs/herod/herod.html)

When Caesar Augustus heard of Herod ordering the murder of his own sons' days before he died, Caesar remarked, *"It would be better to be one of Herod's swine than Herod's son".* In the Greek language a pun was intended using similar sounding terms for son and swine, 'hus', and 'huios'. The insinuation was that Herod being a professed Jew, his pigs were safe from slaughter, but his sons were not.

Archelaus - 2 BC to 1 AD

Archelaus was the elder son of Herod the Great and Malthace the Samaritan. He was therefore one half Idumean and one half Samaritan so he had no Jewish blood in him.

Under Herod the Great's will most of the estates were given to him, together with the title of Ethnarch. His younger brother Antipas II contested the will in Rome. While this was going on there was a time of uncertainty back in Judea, and Archelaus forcibly repressed a rebellion and ordered his soldiers to attack the people.

An estimated 3000 people were killed in this Temple uprising, but the Romans supported him at that time. His harsh government and fiery temper earned him the hatred of his people who formally complained to Rome. He is mentioned only in Matthew 2:22. His reign lasted about three years from 2 BC to 1 AD when Archelaus was finally removed from his position of government, and all his possessions were confiscated and he was banished to Vienna in Gaul for the rest of his life.

Jesus and his parents returned from Egypt to the Holy Land while Archelaus still reigned in Judea. So Jesus was less than 4 years old when they moved to Nazareth.

Herod Antipas II - 2 BC-37 AD

Herod Antipas was the younger son of Herod the Great and Malthace a Samaritan woman so, like his brother, he too was half Idumean and half Samaritan and had no Jewish blood in his body. In considering what to do with this Prince; Caesar Augustus granted him the domain of 'Galilee of the Gentiles', and he ruled as Tetrarch of Galilee from 4 BC to 39 AD.

He first married the daughter of King Aretas of Arabia, however he sent her back to her father the King of Arabia after he had met and seduced his brother Philip's wife, whose name was Herodias. Herodias was the daughter of his half-brother Aristobulus therefore his niece, and also the wife of his other half-brother Philip making his union with her doubly sinful according to the Mosaic Law. After her marriage to him, Herodias totally dominated his life and his influence on his subjects was accordingly likened to yeast or leaven by Jesus in Mark 8:14.

This man was the Herod that John the Baptist preached against for his immorality and lost his life because of his preaching. Pontius Pilate, hearing that Jesus was from Galilee sent him to Herod Antipas II who interviewed him hoping to see a miracle, and then failing that mocked him and sent him back to Pilate. Luke 23:6-12.

In 37 AD Antipas went to Rome to petition for equal kingship with his brother Agrippa at the instigation of his wife Herodias. Agrippa outmaneuvered him in the court at Rome and accused him of high treason. The case dragged on for two years and in AD 39 Antipas was banished to Lyons in Gaul where he lived and died in great poverty and misery.

When sentence was passed upon him Herodias strenuously opposed Caesar and as a result she too was stripped of all her personal wealth and her estates, and sent with him into the same banishment. Josephus the Jewish historian sees this as the judgment of God upon her.

Herod Agrippa I - 9BC – 44 AD

Herod Agrippa I was the son of Aristobulus and his first wife Berenice, and the grandson of Herod the Great. His grandmother was Mariamne the Hasmonean and granddaughter of John Hyrcanus the high priest, so there was a line of Jewish blood in him. He was reputed to strictly keep the Law of Moses. In 37 AD he was made king and given the Tetrarchy of Philip and Lysanius with the added domains of Galilee and Pareara after Antipas' exile in 39 AD.

To please the Jews he slew James the brother of John and imprisoned Peter. He loved popularity and planned Peter's death; but he died himself in the fourth year of his reign during the games at Caesarea. Acts 12 tells of his deeds and death. Josephus tells us that Agrippa on his deathbed said these words; *"I whom you call a God am ordered to depart this life immediately, Providence thus instantly reproves the lying words you just now addressed to me, and I who was by you called immortal am immediately to be hurried away by death".* So the man they called 'Agrippa the Great' came to an untimely end in AD 44, a monument to warn proud men.

Herod Agrippa II - 27 AD – 100 AD

Herod Agrippa II was the last of the race of Herod's. He was the son of Agrippa I and Cypros, his mother, was a grand-niece of Herod the Great. He was 17 years of age at the time of his father's death in AD 44, and thought too young to succeed his father in the kingdom. Six years later in AD 50 the Emperor Claudius conferred on him the Kingdom of Chalcis, and in AD 52 the Tetrarchies of Philip Lysanius together with the title of King. Emperor Nero added the cities of Galilee and Persia to his kingdom in AD 55.

In AD 60 we read the account of Paul pleading before Festus and consulting Agrippa on a point of Jewish law. The last reference in the New Testament to him is found in Acts 25:13 where he comes to salute the Roman governor Festus. He appears in this portion of Scripture in great pomp together with Bernice, his sister, and they were looked upon with great suspicion by the Jewish leaders. At age 73 he died in Rome AD 100 in the third year of Trajan's rule.

28 SIMEON THE JUST

A nd behold, there was a man in Jerusalem, whose name was Simeon" Luke 2:25-35. There are some misconceptions concerning Simeon, due to a misunderstanding of the grammar in the text of Luke's account.

When Luke quotes Simeon as saying in chapter 2:29-30 *"Lord, now lettest thou thy servant depart in peace according to thy word: For mine eyes have seen thy salvation,"* an assumption of old age is made; thinking the speaker is ready to die.

I believe he is saying: 'God has fulfilled the promise that he would live to see the expected One'. In this setting, where Herod had slaughtered a majority of the leaders of his family; there was always a possibility that he could die an early death. Simeon was highly regarded; prominent in society, and one who was a true worshipper of God. He was known for his devotion to the things of God and was in a position of power to dispense Justice.

Adam Clarke comments: "Several learned men are of the opinion that he was son to the famous Hillel, one of the most celebrated doctors and philosophers which had ever appeared in the Jewish nation since the time of Moses. Simeon is supposed also to have been the 'Ab' or president of the grand Sanhedrin". When the Wise Men from the East arrived in Jerusalem, looking for the new born King, Herod, being an Idumean, and not a Jew, called for the Chief Priests and the Scribes for an opinion on where the Messiah would be born. Dr. Lightfoot offers, *"We may therefore guess, and that no improbable conjecture, that, in this assembly, called together by Herod, these were present, among others:-1. Hillel: the president. 2. Shammai: vice-president. 3. The sons of Betira; Judah, and Joshua. 4. Bava Ben Buta. 5. Jonathan the son of Uzziel; the Chaldee paraphrast. 6. Simeon; the son of Hillel"*.

From Lightfoot's calculations Simeon would have been about 31 years of age at the time of the dedication of Baby Jesus. He hears from the Holy Spirit that he is to go to the Nicanor gate in the Temple; and there he finds Joseph, Mary and the Baby Jesus.

Luke 2:27-28 shows Simeon, a priest, later the president of the Sanhedrin, performing the rite of 'Purification of the Parents'; and the dedication of the Baby. In the Hebraic tradition, both the parents had to go through the 'Mikveh' of purification after the birth of a child. Once they had gone through the Mikveh, they were considered ritually clean, the separateness of 'Niddah' was gone, and the mother was no longer 'Tumah' or unclean. Now they could offer the sacrifice and be blessed by the Priest.

Rivkah Slonim in her article on the 'Jewish Woman' explains: *"The status of a Jew - whether he or she was ritually pure or impure - was at the very core of Jewish living; it dictated and regulated a person's involvement in all areas of ritual. Most notably, 'Tumah' made entrance into the Holy Temple impossible and thus sacrificial offering inaccessible".*

This was the ceremony which Simeon performed, ending with his prophecy about both Jesus and Mary.

Simeon was murdered by Herod shortly after this. His tomb has recently been identified close to the eastern wall of the Temple. Simeon, had a son, Gamaliel, who rose to prominence, and became the next leader and teacher of the Law, under whose tutelage Saul of Tarsus and Theophilus, the High Priest, figure in the writings of the New Testament.

29 WISE MEN FROM THE EAST

I
n the Gospel of Matthew 2:1-12 we have the single account of the visit of the "Wise Men" to find the New Born King of Israel. This has been celebrated throughout the church ages as a special event on the church calendar. We are charmed with the picture of these 'Kings' coming to pay homage to the Babe in the Manger! However there is much that is muddled in the minds of Christians concerning this wonderful and true event. There are several questions to consider in connection with this story.

Who were these "Wise Men"?

The word used in the Greek is Mágoi which is the name of a sacred tribe of Priestly men whom the historian Herodotus (1.101) identifies as Median. The Medes were later absorbed by the Persians, but their homeland was 'between the rivers', that is Iraq today.

Joseph Seiss in his book "The Gospel in the Stars" (Kregel 1882) says, "The Magi are specially named in the list of the Median tribes, just as Matthew names them. Anciently they were mostly a pastoral people greatly occupied with religion, astronomy, and other sacred sciences. They were the great teachers of kings and people in the divine wisdom."

Daniel had just completed his studies as a captive in Babylon, when King Nebuchadnezzar dreamed a dream that none could interpret: but Daniel told the King his dream and its interpretation; and was immediately promoted to be chief of the wise men of Babylon. The word 'wise' used in the Chaldee is 'khakkeem' which is a root corresponding to 'Magian' = Wise (Dan. 2:48).

What did they believe?

Quoting Seiss again *"They believed in one God, original Creator, supreme in omniscience and goodness, unrivalled in splendor, and dwelling in light eternal.*

They believed in a great and powerful spirit of evil in constant antagonism to God, the spoiler of the divine works and the author of all mischief."

They also believed that the Constellations of the Stars were given of God to forecast the future and teach man the eternal plan of man's destiny and give him hope. Scholars tell us that Daniel shared with the Magi his people's prophecies regarding a King to be born, that a Star would appear, and based on the revelation given to Daniel, the approximate time they could expect the Messiah (Dan 2:44; Dan 9:25).

What were they looking for?

Mat 2:2 "Where is he that is born king of the Jews?"

There was no doubt in the minds of these men that a king had been born; they simply wished to find and worship Him.

How did they know that a King was born to the Jewish Nation?

It is an astronomic fact that at the precise hour of midnight, at the winter solstice, that is the last week of December the constellation of Virgo, regarded as the virgin mother from whom the divine redeemer king was to be born, was just rising on the eastern horizon. Furthermore at the Spring Equinox, nine months earlier, on the same night and time the stars of the little constellation of 'Como' the special sign of the Infant, the 'Desire of the nations' were on the meridian along with Virgo. At this time there was a conjunction of 2 planets in 'Pisces' the constellation identifying Israel.

It is also recorded in history that a new peculiar star appeared in the constellation 'Como' on the head of the child, and was bright enough to be seen in the daytime. The Chinese record this star at the time of our Savior's birth. This star was on the Meridian nine months before the birth of Christ and again exactly three months after his birth.

There is a reliable story that the wise men journeyed to Bethlehem, six miles from Jerusalem, and camped by the well. This would enable them to take an exact reading of the star, "His Star"; they called it, and found it precisely on the meridian at midnight: by observing the reflection of the star in the water of the well. The vertical sides of the well served them much like an observatory. They determined that 'the star stood over them', that is exactly pinpointing the position, at Bethlehem. Matt. 2:10 says when they saw the star they rejoiced with great joy and entered Bethlehem, and found the house where the young child was.

When did they arrive?

In Luke 2:22 we find that Mary was in the Jerusalem Temple at least 41 days after the birth of Jesus Leviticus 12:2, 4.

Now Matthew 2:11 tells us that "when they were come into the house", not the stable, they fell down and worshipped Him. So some time had elapsed from the birth of our Savior.

In Matthew 2:12 we see that the wise men were warned in a dream to leave by another route, and not to go back to Herod in Jerusalem, then in vs. 13 Joseph is also told in a dream to get out of the country.

It is apparent that at least a month elapsed before the Magi appeared; however most scholars feel it was 3 months later that the wise men arrived. The gifts of the Magi must have come in very useful to them at that time, as they were dirt poor shortly before this; for they offered the gift of the poor in the Temple.

Very little time is given by Josephus between the Massacre of the Babies of Bethlehem and the death of King Herod, but it was some time before the following king was appointed, and he was in office when Joseph and Mary returned to Eretz Israel.

The Bible given by God is accurate, and the Heavens created by God tell the same story, to those who learn its secrets. Certainly the Wise men found the Christ Child by following the Star that pointed to Jesus.

Wise men do well to rejoice when they find Jesus: who was born to take away the sins of the world and reconcile all to the Creator God through dying on the Cross for us.

We would do no better than to bring the offering of our lives to Him.

30 THE MURDER OF ZACHARIAS

Zacharias shattered a Biblical prophetic silence of 400 years at the dedication of his new born son!
"And his father Zacharias was filled with the Holy Spirit, and prophesied." Luke 1:67

No Prophet had spoken in Israel for ten generations. Religious observances continued without impact, until Zacharias proclaimed that God had just set in motion the redemption of Israel. He quoted earlier promises by the ancient prophets, and said that God had remembered His sacred Covenant with Israel. He declared that the baby John would preach repentance from sin, to prepare the way for the coming Messiah; the 'dayspring from on high'. Mary; now three months pregnant with Jesus, was present at that ceremony and hid those inspired words in her heart.

Zacharias was a man of God, and in the last two years of his life he heard personally from God. The Priesthood in the days of Herod had become corrupt; many of them guilty of simony, paying for sacraments and holy offices or for positions in the hierarchy in the Temple. In contrast; Luke tells us that Zacharias and his wife Elizabeth, descended from the Aaronic line, were both true believers, who lived what they believed.

As Zacharias placed the Incense on the Altar; he suddenly became aware of an awesome presence next to him. Looking up, he was shaken to the very core of his being: there stood the Angel Gabriel telling him his prayers had been heard in Heaven, and the child to be born would be the forerunner of the coming Messiah! This was to be the 'Elijah', of Malachi's prophecy, which would turn the hearts of the people back to God. He exited the Temple, unable to speak, and by signs indicated that he had encountered the supernatural during his ministration (Luke 1:22).

Nine months later, family and friends gathered in their home in Hebron, to celebrate the dedication of the new born son; when asked if the child was really to be named John, Zacharias wrote 'His Name is John' on a tablet: at that moment his speech returned to him and he began to prophesy. The miracle of his healing; coupled with the import of his prophecy became widely circulated (Luke 1:66). His wife's cousin Mary, was present and witnessed the naming of the baby John, and heard the prophecy which would impact her life as well. He understood clearly what the Angel had said to him earlier in the Temple: his lifetime of studying the Old Testament was not spent in vain.

The full text of his prophecy is found in Luke 1:67-79. Robertson notes that:

'Nearly every phrase here is found in the Psalms and the Prophets. He . . . was full of the Holy Spirit and had caught the Messianic message in its highest meaning.' - Robertson's Word Pictures.

One year later Zacharias was again on duty in the Temple when an enraged King Herod massacred all the babies less than two years old in Bethlehem. Zacharias was politically knowledgeable and made his plans carefully, sending his wife Elizabeth and their baby John into hiding.

Herod's suspicion was aroused by hearing the story of Zacharias being struck dumb for nine months; then miraculously restored. The miracle of his healing; coupled with the import of his prophecy became widely circulated cf. Luke 1:66. The prophecy the old priest uttered was enough to make Herod think that John might be the Messiah. Taking no chances, Herod sent soldiers to the Temple; demanding Zacharias hand over baby John; they returned to Herod empty-handed. Herod sent them back first thing the next morning with orders to kill the baby or kill Zacharias.

Moments after the soldiers left the Temple, a new work-shift of priests arrived for duty. They called to Zacharias, but there was no reply. One of the priests, walking around the Altar of sacrifice, stopped dead in his tracks; with widening eyes and sweat breaking out on his forehead. At his very feet, a pool of blood was seeping around the corner of the Altar. He took another step forward and there lying between the Altar and the Sanctuary door; was the blood-stained and battered corpse of Zacharias! He had again refused to comply with Herod's demands; so the soldiers killed him there in the sacred temple area, between the Altar and the Holy Place (Protoevangelium of James 23-24).

He had sacrificed his own life to protect his son. He was greatly revered by all and a tomb was constructed just outside the eastern wall of the Temple; wherein he was buried.

In 2003 Joe Zias, an archaeologist with the Israeli Antiquities Authority identified the popularly known 'Yad Avsholom' tomb monument; as that of Zacharias, the father of John the Baptist, which you can see today standing in the Kidron valley[8]. Jesus may well have been referring to this very tomb when He accused the Jews of building "tombs for the prophets and decorating (sic) the monuments of the righteous." Matthew 23:29.

This was the crime that Jesus laid at the feet of the leaders of Israel, saying all their misdeeds from Abel's murder to that of Zacharias would be accounted for in their generation. The ISV translation says; "will happen to those living today." Jesus died about AD 32: and the Romans destroyed Jerusalem and the Temple in AD 70; less than forty years later.

The 'Herods' of this world may silence the messenger; but they can never silence the message. The message of God's forgiveness and love towards sinful men has transformed people and nations. We divide history between BC and AD because of the impact of Jesus' birth.

People who heard from God back then, were no different from people today. Zacharias, Elizabeth, Mary and Joseph all acted on what God told them. Obedience to what God showed them, through Angels, dreams and visions resulted in the incredible events that we celebrate as Christmas. Zacharias shattered a Biblical prophetic silence of 400 years at the dedication of his new born son!

8

www.biblesearchers.com/hebrewchurch/archaeology/zachariasimeon.s
html

31 THE FAMILY OF JESUS

In smaller communities it is normal that everyone knows all about everyone else. When Jesus returned to His hometown and began teaching the people in their synagogue, they were amazed and began to question among themselves. Matthew records in Chapter 13:54 - 56, the questions that were flung about by the locals who had grown up around Jesus.

These questions tell us a lot about who Jesus was!
"Where did this man get this wisdom and these miracles? vs. 54
"This is the builder's son, isn't it?
His mother is named Mary, isn't she?
His brothers are James, Joseph, Simon, and Judas, aren't they?" vs.55
"And his sisters are all with us, aren't they?" vs.56

It is significant that on His return to Nazareth, after the endowment of the Holy Spirit during His baptism by John the Baptist, He was noticeably different in the eyes of the Villagers of Nazareth. They now question how He could possibly accomplish the miracles; and have such wisdom. This debunks the fables of Jesus performing miracles as a child in Nazareth!

They now begin to state known facts about Him, and his familial relationships.
1. He was the son of a builder (ISV) or Carpenter (KJV).
2. His mother was Mary.
3. He had 4 brothers; the Greek word is 'Adelphos' from the womb of Mary.
4. He had at least 3 sisters; Greek = 'Adelphe' female from the womb, of Mary.

If he had but one sister, they would have said so. If he had two; the word in the Greek would be 'both'. Here they refer to all, being three or more; who were currently all living in the vicinity of Nazareth at the time, and known to the locals.

In Psa. 69:8 there is a prophetic verse that points to Jesus; saying: *"I have become a stranger to my brothers and an alien to my mother's children;"* This strongly suggests that Jesus mother would have children after His birth.

There is a school of thought that suggests Joseph had other children before marrying Mary, but this makes no sense in the clear fact that these known ones are called His siblings and followed Mary to Capernaum to hinder his ministry Matthew 12:46-47. This is the plain sense of this account.

In the earlier years of Church history, there was an attempt to deify Mary, and liken her to the pagan female deity, who is supposed to be the mother of a divine son, and who is yet a virgin. This female goddess was known in different countries variously: in Egypt as Isis; Cybele in Rome; Isi in Asia; Fortuna in Greece and Shing Moo in China.

Mary said of herself: *"Behold the handmaid of the Lord"* Luke *1:38*. Here handmaid Gk. 'doule' means slave girl. *"And she brought forth her firstborn son"* Luke 2:7. Greek - 'prototokos' is a word used to indicate other children followed.

If she had an only son, the word would have been 'monogenes' used in Luke 7:12; 8:42. The 'monogenes' title is used of Jesus being God's only son in John 1:14, 18. God only had one son, and that by Mary, but Mary had many children, after the birth of Jesus, by Joseph; 4 sons, and 3 or more daughters, known to the populace as Joseph and Mary's children and Brothers and Sisters of Jesus, though in fact they were half-brothers and half-sisters, as Joseph was not Jesus father, but adoptive father.

Jesus said we are to search the Scriptures and see that they speak of Him. It pays to study the Bible and cross reference these facts, before believing every tradition put out by those who seek their own agenda.

32 JESUS MESSIANIC LINEAGE

It is easy for people to imagine a contradiction in the Bible when they read the accounts of Jesus lineage in Matthew and Luke's Gospels. I believe there are no contradictions in the Word of God.

What we have here is double occurrence of the Jewish law designed for the continuance of inheritance.

"Her husband's brother shall go in unto her, and take her to him to wife, and perform the duty of a husband's brother unto her. And it shall be that the first-born that she beareth shall succeed in the name of his brother that is dead, that his name be not blotted out of Israel." Deuteronomy 25:5-6 ASV

Let's find the references in the Gospels:

"Eliud begat Eleazar; and Eleazar begat Matthan; and Matthan begat Jacob; and Jacob begat Joseph the husband of Mary, of whom was born Jesus, who is called Christ." Matthew 1:15-16

"And Jesus himself, when he began to teach, was about thirty years of age, being the son (as was supposed) of Joseph, the son of Heli, the son of Matthat, the son of Levi, the son of Melchi," Luke 3:23-24

Smith's Bible Dictionary explains Mat'that, *(gift of God)* is another form of the name Matthan.

I recently came across the writings of Solomon of Akhlat, a bishop of Basrah, Iraq during the thirteenth century. His 'Book of the Bee', was a collection of Jewish records and teachings. In the 33rd chapter discussing the Messianic Generations, he explains the Genealogies of Mary and Joseph.

"Mattan the son of Eliezer-whose descent was from the family of Solomon-took a wife whose name was Astha (or Essetha) and by her begat Jacob naturally. Mattan died, and Melchi, whose family descended from Nathan the son of David, took her to wife, and begat by her Eli (or Heli); hence Jacob and Heli are brothers, the sons of one mother.

"Eli (or Heli) took a wife and died without children. Then Jacob, his brother took her to wife, to raise up seed to his brother, according to the command of the law; and he begat by her Joseph, who was the son of Jacob according to nature, but the son of Heli according to the law; so whichever ye choose, whether according to nature, or according to the law, Christ is found to be the son of David.

"It is moreover right to know that Eliezer begat two sons, Mattan and Jotham. Mattan begat Jacob; and Jacob begat Joseph. Jotham begat Zadok, and Zadok begat Mary. From this it is clear that Joseph's father and Mary's father were cousins."

Mattan was the grandfather of the Virgin Mary. She and Joseph were also second cousins. So when someone tells you there are contradictions in the Bible, take time to look deeper than the surface, and you will find there is an explanation that is sometimes not apparent at the first glance. You really can trust the Word of God.

Quotes are taken from the Bible ASV, and the Book of the Bee, translated by E. A. Wallis Budge, M.A. Oxford, The Clarendon Press 1886.

33 THE THREE JAMES' IN THE GOSPELS

There are three men in the New Testament closely associated with Jesus of Nazareth, who are called by the name of James. The Greek uses the word Jacob, from which the name James in English is a derivative.

It can become confusing to one who has not carefully studied the familial relationships of each of these men, and even some Biblical commentators have become confused, further blurring the understanding of who each one was. These are:

James, the son of Zebedee,
James the Less,
James, the half-brother of Jesus.

It is easy to get mixed up, doing a superficial reading of the New Testament, and not determining the details concerning these three. Let's look at each one, with the Scripture references, as to their family.

 # 1 James, the son of Zebedee

This James is called the son of Zebedee and the brother of John. He worked with his father and brother as a fisherman Matthew 4:21. His mother seems to have been Salome, as a comparison of Matt 27:56 and Mark 16:1 imply. Jesus called him directly from his fishing boat, to be one of the 12 Apostles Matt 10:2. The fact of his name appearing first before his brother John, gives some credence to the theory that he was the older of the two. He was singled out to be part of an 'inner circle' among the disciples.

He was present at the raising of Jairus' daughter from the dead Mark 5:37; the Transfiguration of Jesus Mark 9:2-8; the Agony in the Garden of Gethsemane Mark 14:32-41, and was furious at the rejection of Jesus by the people of Samaria; wanting to call down lightning to strike them Luke 9:54-55.

On the road to Jerusalem, this James and his brother John asked for preferential seating on either side of Jesus in the Kingdom Mark 10:35-40.

James sat on the Mount of Olives with Jesus and asked Jesus to explain the end-times events and the destruction of Jerusalem of which Jesus had just taught them Mark 13:3. James was in the Boat with John and Peter fishing, when Jesus appeared to them after His resurrection John 21:1-6.

James was murdered by Herod Agrippa I in about AD 44; almost 11 years after Jesus death Acts 12:1-2. Thus was fulfilled the prophecy of Jesus in Mark 10:39 to the effect that James would indeed drink of the cup of suffering like Jesus, dying a violent death. This basically is the outline of the person and life of James the son of Zebedee.

2 James, the Less

Here we have the second James. He too is listed as an Apostle in Matt 10:3. This is extremely important to keep in mind, as you begin to read the book of Acts. He is designated "James the Less" in Mark 15:40, and we are told that his mother's name was Mary. A parallel scripture in John 19:25, tells us that this Mary was the wife of Cleopas, or Alphaeus, as he is also called. Mark 3:18 tells us his father was Alphaeus. Tradition suggests Alphaeus was the brother of Joseph. This would make James the Less' mother, Mary, and Mary the mother of Jesus, sisters-in-law.

We should take careful note there were only two Apostles named James.

After the death of James the son of Zebedee we find James the Less is the only Apostle with that name still alive. That he is related to the Lord Jesus through kinship of his father Alphaeus to Joseph; makes him a cousin to Jesus. In the tribal cultures of the Middle East and Africa, the term 'Brother' is still used for close relatives, such as cousins.

In Acts 12:1-2 James son of Zebedee is killed, and in vs.17 Peter after being delivered from Prison by an Angel, arrives at the home of Mary, John Mark's mother, and tells the believers to inform James and the Brethren. James can only be this Apostle and a son of Alphaeus. James the son of Zebedee was already dead, and Peter knew it.

When Paul went up to Jerusalem, Luke relates that he met only with the Apostles, Peter and James Gal 1:19, and the term here makes it clear that James was an Apostle; but also had some blood relationship to Jesus. James is clearly now the leader of the Church in Jerusalem Acts 15:13-19, and he is listed first in Gal 2:9 with Peter and John as the leaders of the Jerusalem Church. The reference to Jesus appearing to James has been applied to mean his physical half-brother; but the scripture itself indicates that it was James the Apostle 1Cor 15:7.

It seems clear that the Epistle of James was authored by the leader of the Church in Jerusalem, who does not claim to be anything but a servant of God and of the Lord Jesus Christ. His letter is impersonal, and such as would be expected by the leader of the Church in Jerusalem, to the people dispersed among other nations. It is an apostolic letter to the people of God, with teaching on Christian Conduct and Life style. We have to conclude that this was written by James the son of Alphaeus.

I found a comment in the International Standard Bible Encyclopedia that quotes Hegesippus, a Jewish Christian in the middle of the second century, as saying

"James was often in the temple praying for forgiveness for the people. At the Passover shortly before the destruction of Jerusalem (foretold in his epistle, James 5:1) the scribes and Pharisees set him on a pinnacle of the temple, and begged him to restrain the people who were "going astray after Jesus as though He were the Christ." "Tell us, O just one," said they before the assembled people, "which is the door of Jesus?" alluding to his prophecy "the coming of the Lord draweth nigh ... behold the Judge standeth before the doors" (Greek, James 5:8-9), wherein he repeats Jesus' words (Mat 24:33), "when ye shall see all these things, know that He (margin) is near, even at the doors." James replied with a loud voice, "Why ask ye me concerning Jesus, the Son of Man? He sitteth at the right hand of power, and will come again on the clouds of heaven." Many cried "Hosanna to the Son of David."

But James was cast down by the Pharisees. Praying, "Father, forgive them, for they know not what they do," he was stoned in spite of the remonstrance of a Rechabite priest ("Stop! The just one is praying for you!"), then beaten to death with a fuller's club. Thus the Jews wreaked their vengeance on him, exasperated at his prophecy of their national doom in his epistle, which was circulated not only in Jerusalem but by those who came up to the great feasts, among "the twelve tribes scattered abroad" to whom it is addressed. Josephus makes Ananus, the high priest after Festus' death, to have brought James before the Sanhedrin for having broken the laws, and to have delivered him and some others to be stoned.

His apprehension by Ananus was very probably in this year; but according to Hegesippus he was not martyred until just before the destruction of Jerusalem, A.D. 69. James the Just, the leader of the church in Jerusalem, was thrown over a hundred feet down from the southeast pinnacle of the Temple

when he refused to deny his faith in Christ. When they discovered that he survived the fall, his enemies beat James to death with a fuller's club. This was the same pinnacle where Satan had taken Jesus during the Temptation."

In this way James: the son of Alphaeus; brother of Matthew (Levi); and writer of the Epistle of James, came to his tragic end.

3 James, the Brother of Jesus

The third James is shown to be the son of Mary, wife of Joseph, and known well to the people of Nazareth and the region around there Matt 12:46, Mark 3:21.

There is a strong teaching in the Roman Catholic Church that Mary had no other children. However the context of the Gospel Story makes clear that Jesus had brothers and sisters who were not believers in Him. The oldest of these sons appears to be also called James.

Matthew 1:16 shows that Joseph's father was named Jacob, also translated James. It is frequently customary to name a first born son after the father or grandfather. Joseph and Mary were commanded by the Angel to name their first child Jesus. When the next child came along it would be natural to name him either Joseph or James (Jacob).

As writer of this article, I have the honor of bearing the name of James, and am named after five previous generations of James. I work with a fine man, who has the first name of George. His family lists enough Georges among them to cause those of us who know them to have to think carefully who we are referring to!

It is apparent that Mary, Jesus mother, remained in the circle of Believers, as we find her a participant, on the day of Pentecost Acts 1:14. As Jesus was dying on the Cross, He entrusted John the son of Zebedee with the care of his mother Mary as we see in John 19:26-27, and not to his half-brother James.

When care is taken to peruse the Scriptures, I am not sure that the half-brother of Jesus ever became a believer. The scriptures quoted to bolster this theory, are based on the assumption of the word brethren being narrow in its application, whereas in many places Jesus himself uses the broader application.

34 A MAN GOD USED

He was a P.K. Yes a Preachers Kid! His Dad was a minister and his Mom was in Church regularly. They told him that when he was born God showed them he would be a Preacher too, and be used mightily by the Lord. His friends called him Jay.

He grew up to manhood, with a sense of destiny. At age 31 he had prepared himself to preach a message of repentance, and he began his ministry. He went to the Western edge of the Hashemite Kingdom of Jordan. In this somewhat hostile environment he began to gather a congregation around him. The attendance at his meetings began to grow with each passing week.

It did not take long for the word to get out about this fiery Evangelist, and his audiences comprised many common people seeking to get right with God.

The Academia also came to listen to him, and many of the Politicians and leading ministers were present to critique his sermons. It did not faze him one bit. Jay just kept on with his scorching messages against hypocrisy and injustice, against wickedness in high places, and he pulled no punches!

He had been preaching about a year or more when he heard that the State Governor had divorced his wife and seduced a married woman to leave her husband and marry him. This was grist to the Preacher's mill, and he publicly and loudly rebuked the Governor for his disgraceful conduct. The Governor was furious and arranged to have Jay assassinated. This was speedily carried out.

The people of the land grieved for Jay, and looked back on his anointed ministry for years after that. Yes this Jewish evangelist had impacted the entire community where he had so fearlessly preached the message of repentance.

Jay was known by his full name among his own people: *"Johanan Ben-Zacharias Cohen"*. Perhaps you do not know his story or recognize his name? He does have a contemporary nick-name that you might recognize. It is "John the Baptist".

35 JOHN THE BAPTIST

The sources of first-hand information concerning the life and work of John the Baptist are limited to the New Testament and Josephus. John's Gospel deals chiefly with John after the baptism of Jesus. Josephus makes an interesting reference to the cause of John's imprisonment, saying that Herod was influenced to put John to death by the:

"Fear lest his great influence over the people might put it in his power or inclination to raise a rebellion. Accordingly, he was sent a prisoner, out of Herod's suspicious temper, to Macherus, and was there put to death." (*Ant.,* XVIII, v, 2)

This account of Josephus does not necessarily conflict with the tragic story of the Gospels. If Herod desired to punish or destroy him for the reasons assigned by the evangelists, he would doubtless wish to offer as the public reason some political charge, and the one named by Josephus would be near at hand.

John was of priestly descent in the line of Aaron, and his father, Zacharias, was a priest of the course of Abia; and did service in the temple at Jerusalem at a certain time each year. King David had divided the Priests into 24 groups or courses, as they had become so numerous, and each group were assigned a certain time to do duty in the Temple at Jerusalem. Luke says of Zacharias and his wife, that: *"They were both righteous before God, walking in all the commandments and ordinances of the Lord blameless"* (Luke 1:6).

This priestly ancestry is in interesting contrast with John's prophetic work. John grew up in strict Levitical training. This is seen in the light of the Angel's announcement *"Many shall rejoice at his birth. For he shall be great in the sight of the Lord, and he shall drink no wine nor strong drink; and he shall be filled with the Holy Spirit, even from his mother's womb"* Luke 1:14-16.

In Luke's brief statement we read: "And the child grew, and waxed strong in spirit, and was in the deserts till the day of his showing unto Israel" Luke 1:80.

The International Standard Bible Encyclopedia points out that: *"John's dress and habits were strikingly suggestive of Elijah, the old prophet of national judgment. His desert habits have led some to connect him with that strange company of Jews known as the Essenes. There is, however, little foundation for such a connection other than his ascetic habits and the fact that the chief settlement of this sect was near the home of his youth. It was natural that he should continue the manner of his youthful life in the desert, and it is not improbable that he intentionally copied his great prophetic model. It was fitting that the one who called men to repentance and the beginning of a self-denying life should show renunciation and self-denial in his own life. But there is no evidence in his teaching that he required such asceticism of those who accepted his baptism."*

As a preacher, John was eminently practical and discriminating. Self-love and covetousness were the prevalent sins of the people at large. On them, therefore, he enjoined charity and consideration for others. The publicans he cautioned against extortion, the soldiers against crime and plunder. His doctrine and manner of life roused the entire south of Palestine, and the people from all parts flocked to the place where he preached; on the banks of the Jordan River. There he baptized thousands unto repentance. John was aware that his baptism was a preparation for the Messianic baptism anticipated by the prophets, who saw that for a true cleansing, the nation must wait until God should open in Israel a fountain for cleansing as prophesied in Zacharias 13:1. His baptism was at once a preparation and a promise of the spiritual cleansing which the Messiah would bestow.

"I indeed baptize you with water unto repentance: but he that cometh after me ... shall baptize you with the Holy Spirit and with fire" Matt. 3:11.

After Jesus had been baptized John realized that his task was done and said that Jesus must increase and he, John, must decrease (John 3:30) John had found his divine purpose in life and fulfilled it. Jesus made it clear that John's life was not wasted.

"Truly I say to you, among those who have been born of women there has not risen a greater one than John the Baptist. But the least in the kingdom of Heaven is greater than he" Mat 11:11.

Like John you may not understand the circumstances and current events around you; but you can rest in the same answer that Jesus gave to John. When you keep eternal values in view you will not fail.

36 WHAT HAPPENED TO JOHN'S HEAD?

John the Baptist was the son of a Priest, a Cohen, and his father was Zacharias; so his proper full name was not 'John the Baptist', but Johanan Ben Zacharias Cohen.

" *For Herod himself had sent and laid hold of John, and bound him in prison for the sake of Herodias, his brother Philip's wife; for he had married her. Because John had said to Herod, "It is not lawful for you to have your brother's wife." Therefore Herodias held it against him and wanted to kill him, but she could not; for Herod feared John, knowing that he was a just and holy man, and he protected him. And when he heard him, he did many things, and heard him gladly. Then an opportune day came when Herod on his birthday gave a feast for his nobles, the high officers, and the chief men of Galilee. And when Herodias' daughter herself came in and danced, and pleased Herod and those who sat with him, the king said to the girl, "Ask me whatever you want, and I will give it to you." He also swore to her, "Whatever you ask me, I will give you, up to half my kingdom." So she went out and said to her mother, "What shall I ask?" And she said, "The head of John the Baptist!" Immediately she came in with haste to the king and asked, saying, "I want you to give me at once the head of John the Baptist on a platter." And the king was exceedingly sorry; yet, because of the oaths and because of those who sat with him, he did not want to refuse her. Immediately the king sent an executioner and commanded his head to be brought. And he went and beheaded him in prison, brought his head on a platter, and gave it to the girl; and the girl gave it to her mother.". Mark 6:17-28 - NKJV.*

Now Herod Antipas II, also known as Herod the Tetrarch was the son of Herod the Great by Malthace, a Samaritan. His first wife was the daughter of Aretas of Damascus, King of Arabia Peraea, but Herod sent her back to her father, and took Herodias, the wife of his half-brother Herod Philip as his wife.

King Aretas ruled the City of Damascus, at the time of the death of John the Baptist and was still living when Paul was converted.

"In Damascus the governor, under Aretas the king was guarding the city of the Damascenes with a garrison, desiring to arrest me;" 2 Corinthians 11:32.

"Herod beheaded John the Baptist for criticizing his relationship with Herodias, his Brother Philip's wife. King Aretas who was indignant at the insult offered to his daughter next threatened war against Herod. It would appear that this was the occasion when Herod Antipas II sent the head of John the Baptist to King Aretas in Damascus; as a warning of what happens to those who crossed him. Aretas, then commanded his Army to fight with Herod Antipas' Army, and defeated him with great loss. (Josephus Book 18, Ch. 5.)

"This defeat, according to the famous passage in Josephus, was attributed by many to the murder of John the Baptist, which had been committed by Antipas shortly before, under the influence of Herodias". (Mat.14:4 ff; Mar. 6:17 ff; Luke 3:19;" Smith's Bible Dictionary).

The head of John the Baptist thus was brought to Damascus where a thriving Christian Church was in existence; and the people all revered John the Baptist as a Prophet. John's head was placed in an ornate gilded Sepulcher, in the Church that became known as the "Cathedral of Saint John the Baptist." This building changed hands several times during the centuries, and in 1966 it was the Great Umayyad Muslim Mosque which still held the Shrine; allegedly containing the Head of John. I personally visited there in 1966. My Muslim guide asserted that the head was there; but no one questioned the fact that this was indeed the shrine of the head of John the Baptist.

Herod Antipas was banished to Lyons in Gaul (France) where he lived and died in great poverty and misery. When sentence was passed upon him Herodias strenuously opposed the angry Caesar, and as a result, she too was stripped of all her personal wealth and her estates; and sent with him into the same banishment. Josephus, the Jewish historian, sees this as the judgment of God upon her.

37 THE MAN IN THE SHADOWS

In the Gospel of Luke we are told of Jesus and His disciples going from the Last Supper to the Garden of Gethsemane, where they all slept, and left Jesus to pray alone. We are told that He prayed three times, and much of what He actually prayed; that he sweat great drops of blood; and that an Angel appeared to Him and strengthened Him. Luke 22:43–45. The question that comes to mind is; who recorded these happenings if the disciples were all asleep?

My answer to you is; the Man in the Shadows!

"Now a certain young man followed Him, having a linen cloth thrown around his naked body, and the young men laid hold of him, and he left the linen cloth and fled from them naked." Mark 14:51-52.

He is not one of the 12 disciples but the Bible gives us clues to his identity. We are told he followed them from the guest house, literally an Inn, which the Disciples Peter and John, had found by Jesus instructions to follow a young man carrying a pitcher of water. Luke 22:10. Men did not do that in that culture, so it was unusual enough for the disciples to know this was the one to follow.

Then they came to the house and asked for the 'guest chamber' Mar 14:14 according to Jesus instructions. The word in the Greek 'Kataluma' is used of a lodging house for travelers, i.e. an Inn. This young man was working there, and followed Jesus to Gethsemane. This place became the headquarters for the disciples.

"Then they returned to Jerusalem from the mount called Olivet, which is near Jerusalem, a Sabbath day's journey, and when they had entered, they went up into the upper room where they were staying". In Acts 1:12-13. The Amplified version adds 'indefinitely'

After an Angel delivered Peter out of the Prison (Act 12:12), he went to the house of Mary the mother of John, whose surname was Mark, where a large number were assembled together and were praying. Now we are told that the house belonged to Mary the mother of John Mark. So it would appear the young water carrier, and eavesdropper, of the Gethsemane events was young John whose surname was Mark.

John Mark is led to Jesus

The Disciples stayed there and from the reference in 1Pe 5:13, it is believed that Peter actually led John Mark to the Lord as his personal savior. Peter writes years later: "Your sister church in Babylon, chosen by God, *and my son Mark* send you greetings". The tern 'my son' is used of ones led to faith in Jesus.

What became of John Mark?

Acts 15:37 tells us that John Mark was a relative (the Nephew) of Barnabas. His Mother Mary maintained the Hostel, with the Upper Room where Jesus and his entourage stayed in Jerusalem. Paul and Barnabas visited there and returned to Antioch, and took John Mark with them. His last name was Roman, and they must have felt he could help them work among the Gentiles (Acts 12:25).

John Mark was chosen to join the Missionary team

"*And when they arrived in Salamis, they preached the word of God in the synagogues of the Jews. They also had John as their assistant.*" *Acts 13:4-5*. Note: their assistant = Greek 'huperetes'- Under Oarsman - one who does the hardest work, in the lowest level of the ship.

John Mark deserts Paul and Barnabas

"*Now Paul and his companions sailed from Paphos and came to Perga in Pamphylia. And John Mark separated himself from them and went back to Jerusalem" Acts 13:13*

He was likely fed up with the position he was put in; and the preeminence Paul gained over his uncle Barnabas.

John Mark becomes a bone of contention between two leaders

Paul and Barnabas return to Antioch; then they consider another trip.

"*Then after some days Paul said to Barnabas, "Let us now go back and visit our brethren in every city where we have preached the word of the Lord, and see how they are doing. Now Barnabas wanted to take with them John called Mark [his near relative]. But Paul did not think it best to have along with them the one who had quit and deserted them in Pamphylia and had not gone on with them to the work.*

And there followed a sharp disagreement between them, so that they separated from each other, and Barnabas took Mark with him and sailed away to Cyprus" Acts 15:36-39 Amplified Version.

Paul changes his mind about John Mark

There have often been controversies between strong leaders. A good leader is one who is willing to change his mind when he sees he was wrong. It took time, but Paul finally acknowledged that John Mark was committed to the work of the ministry and could be relied upon after becoming mature. He wrote to Timothy requesting he recruit John Mark to their team.

"Luke alone is with me. Get Mark and bring him with you, for he is very helpful to me for the ministry." 2Timothy 4:11

So John Mark, the man in the Shadows, went from:

Curiosity to Christianity,

Mischief to Missionary,

Deserter to Disciple,

Manhood to Maturity,

Finally Paul who had rejected him in the beginning, calls him a fellow-worker in Philemon 1:24.

This impulsive young man who stood in the Shadows of the Olive trees in Gethsemane, as a young fellow, went on to serve Jesus all his life. It was John Mark who heard Jesus prayers, while the only other three within earshot were sleeping; and it was he who witnessed the Angelic visitation in Gethsemane.

We have him to thank for keeping a record of Jesus prayers during His agony. When you read the Gospel of Mark, you are reading the book authored by John Mark!

Bends in your road, can lead to a productive life for the Lord. For every one of us on our Spiritual Journey, there will be times of failure and frustration, but under the care of concerned mentors and loving fellow Christians, we have the prospect of growth and maturity and ultimately productive ministry in the Kingdom of God.

We need to be patient and keep our gaze on Jesus. If we are sincere the Lord will work out the details, and around the bend in the road will be a glorious end, as you hear your Lord say; "Well done good and faithful servant".

38 WHO WAS THE OTHER JUDAS?

A *Servant:* JUDE LEBBAEUS, THADDAEUS. Jude calls himself "servant of Jesus Christ, and brother of James"

An Apostle:

"And when it was day, he called unto him his disciples: and of them he chose twelve, whom also he named apostles; . . . and Judas the brother of James, and Judas Iscariot, which also was the traitor." Luke 6:13, 16.

Luke and John writing later, when no confusion with Judas Iscariot was likely, call him simply "Judas."

The James referred to in the scriptures is James the Less.

Their father Alpheus, sometimes called Cleopas, was reputedly the brother of Joseph, the husband of Mary the Mother of Jesus. In that respect they were cousins of the Lord Jesus in the eyes of the people of their day. It was James the Less who became the leader of the Church in Jerusalem, and was for many years revered by the Christian Church.

It is important to know that James the son of Zebedee was killed by Herod just before Peter was arrested and miraculously delivered from prison by an angel. Jude therefore, not so well known as an Apostle, references his well-known brother James, in order to introduce himself in his epistle.

An Enquirer:

The primary Biblical notice of him speaking is in John 14:22, where, not understanding Jesus' promise of verse 21, Judas (not Iscariot) asked "Lord, how is it that Thou wilt manifest Thyself unto us and not unto the world?"

A Pentecostal Participant:

He is listed as one of those in the Upper Room, in Acts 1:14 He was a witness to the resurrection of Jesus from the dead; and of Jesus ascension into heaven; and filled with the Holy Spirit on the Day of Pentecost.

A Penman:

Matthew Henry writes: "He that in Mark was called Thaddeus, in Matthew Lebbaeus, whose surname was Thaddeus, is here called Judas the brother of James, the same that wrote the epistle of Jude."

A Prophetic Proclamation

Jude in verses 17-18 reminds believers *"of the words spoken before of the apostles of our Lord Jesus; how they told you that there should be mockers in the last time that should walk after their own ungodly lusts".*

Jude is here quoting Peter's second letter in chapter 3:2-3. Peter's predictive statements become, some years later in Jude; current conditions of which Jude has been informed. Jude writes to the believers affected by this condition, actually referring back to the second epistle of Peter.

It is interesting to see that Jude in his letter quotes eleven times from Second Peter. Jude's message to the Church is urgent, and forceful; pointing out that Peter's prophecy of 2 Peter 2:1 has come true.

"There shall be false teachers among you, who privily shall bring in damnable heresies, even denying the Lord that bought them, and bring upon themselves swift destruction."

The International Bible Encyclopedia gives a detailed Description of the Libertines and Apostates.

"It is needful to gaze with steady vision on the portrait Jude furnishes of these depraved foes, if we are to appreciate in any measure the force of his language and the corruption already wrought in the brotherhood. Some of their foul teachings and their vicious practices, not all, are here set down."

It is well worth reading their detailed list. We can learn much from this, as the Church today is being invaded with old apostate and libertine doctrines; by which many people without knowledge of history are being deceived.

The Ministry

Jude was accounted as one who preached in Mesopotamia, as Jerome remarks in his comments on the Gospel of Matthew. Mesopotamia was an area to which many Christians moved after the outbreak of the persecution of Christians by the Romans.

Tradition connects him with the foundation of the church at Edessa (Smiths Bible Dict.). The exact date of the introduction of Christianity into Edessa in northern Mesopotamia is not certain. Seleucus I Nicator, re-founded the town as a military colony in 303 BC, and called it Edessa; it became the Capital city of the region known as Armenia. However there is no doubt that even before AD 190 Christianity had spread vigorously within Edessa and its surroundings and that the royal house joined the church.

History records that a Christian council was held at Edessa as early as 197 AD. Hegesippus recounted "when Emperor Domitian inquired after David's posterity, grandsons of Jude "the Lord's brother" were brought before him; they stated their possessions were 39 acres, and that they paid him taxes there out and lived by labor, pointing as a proof to their hard hands". They added: "Christ's kingdom is not of this world, but heavenly, and will be manifested when He shall come again in glory."

Certainly the early Christians were taught to be law abiding, and to work well; so that the Name of Christ should be held in honor by Unbelievers. Jude's final admonition applies to us today.

"But ye, beloved, building up yourselves on your most holy faith, praying in the Holy Ghost, Keep your selves in the love of God, looking for the mercy of our Lord Jesus Christ unto eternal life." Jude 1:20-21.

39 A WOMAN WITH A PAST

The setting sun shone warmly on her back as she left the city and headed for the nearby village. It was late afternoon, and the trees and grasses were displaying their best spring garb, as the birds warbled their mating calls and sang their joyous songs of sheer exuberance.

Mary walked with purpose in her stride. She knew there was a banquet scheduled in the village where her brother and sister lived, and she had decided that she would enter that dining hall with her most treasured possession in her arms. It had cost her a year's income to buy it, and now she no longer had the earnings that had come to her in the past. How she would support herself in the future, she did not know, but a change had come about in her life; and she owed a debt of gratitude to the only man who saw her as a person, and not as something to be used.

She knew they had intentionally not invited her to the banquet; her reputation was all too well known in both the city and the village. She had been a member of the oldest profession in the world, until just recently. Her beauty and poise had brought the rich and the powerful men of the city to her door, and she had prospered while ignoring the public slights and contempt of those who were not averse to visiting her on a dark night. She had little use for the religion they professed; while they lived by a double standard.

As she started up the slope toward the village, her breath came a little faster with the exertion. Her brother and sister would likely be there. Simon's son would be there too; she made a face as she thought of him. They had both been teenagers together in the village, but there was something about him that repelled her. He had never been quite honest; some of her friends had also questioned his integrity.

133

Well she would ignore him; after all she was done with the old life.

She knew the Master was to be the guest of honor there. This was her one chance to publicly honor the man whose counsel had helped her turn away from her sinful life, and find forgiveness and peace for her inner being.

The village of Bethany came into view as she crested the rise, the stone walls of the houses giving off the golden glow of a setting sun. The air here was fresh, and clean; not like the city smells of garbage and decay. She stopped a moment, savoring the view. Yes, there was the Big House. She had always called it that; the wealthy Pharisee Simon's house.

Simon had for several years been excluded from the community as a leper. His son had taken care of the business, importing and selling dates from their palm groves down in Kerioth; a day's walk south of Hebron. Now Simon was home again these past three years; since his meeting with the Master in Galilee. He had been healed, and was again being called Simon the Pharisee, instead of Simon the leper.

Mary wondered about that. She had never heard of a miracle of healing like that before, but there was no doubt that Simon was well now. It was then that Simon's son left home. Seems there was a story about the business records not being what his father Simon expected, and Judas had been sent to the Master. She doubted the Master could change Judas, and as for the rumor that he was now treasurer for the group, well that was looking for trouble, she thought.

She looked over towards her sister Martha's house; there was no smoke rising from the cooking area, so yes, Martha was probably catering for Simon's banquet. She wondered if the old skinflint would remunerate her sister; or just take her for granted as had so often happened in the past.

It was time to make her move, so she stepped in with her head held high, and her gift in her arms. The meal was now in progress, Martha directing the servants as the food was served. She hoped fervently that Martha would not interfere with her again this time.

Mary looked over the guests. There was Simon in his robes and tassels, sitting with several of the dignitaries and chief priests from the city. Mary saw her brother, Lazarus, sitting at the table. She felt deep emotion as she looked at him. It was just a short time ago that the Master had simply spoken aloud at the grave side, and Lazarus had come alive, after having been dead four days! That was the one thing that convinced her that the Master was for real.

Her heart swelled within her, she felt tears forming, so yes, she must make her gift, no matter what it cost; and do it now. Mary stepped around the perimeter of the hall, towards the Master, when suddenly she intercepted the malevolent gaze of Judas, Simon's son. She shrugged and continued until she stood behind Jesus, then breaking the seal on her Alabaster box, she poured some of the ointment on his feet and as the tears began to stream down her face she bent and wiped them from his feet with her hair.

Simon, the Pharisee, cast a piercing look at her, but then Jesus interrupted him to tell a story, about two debtors, and asked Simon who loved the most when their debts were forgiven. Jesus then deliberately turned to Mary, and said, *"Your sins are forgiven. Your faith has saved you; go in peace."*

At this point Judas initiated a protest, soon joined by the other disciples, of what he called, her waste!

Instantly Jesus publicly and sternly, rebuked Judas in front of Simon, his own father. To be treated like this was the final straw. He had hoped to embarrass Mary; now he was the one who had lost face. This was the time to make his move. Judas rose from his place and stepped over to where the two chief priests were eating, and stealthily arranged to betray Jesus his Master, for the price of a slave.

Mary quietly left the banquet and walked away, taking the road back to the city. She now saw a bright future ahead. She had found unconditional forgiveness and would forever be a follower of the Master; no matter what happened. It felt like she had been born all over again.

Biblical References: Matt 26:6-13, Mark 1:40, 3:13,19, 14:3-9, Luke 7:36-50, 10:40, John 11:1,14,17,43, 12:1-8.

40 SIMON'S SON

Simon is a name that is found frequently in the annals of the Scripture, and several Simons are mentioned in the New Testament.

There is Simon Peter; Simon the Tanner of Joppa; Simon Zelotes, one of the 12 apostles; and Simon, the brother of Jesus; Simon, ('the Black man'= Niger) of Cyrene in N. Africa; Simon the Pharisee/Leper; and Simon Magus, a Samaritan.

Who was Simon of Bethany? Matt. 26:6.

Here we are looking at the Simon who is clearly identified as a Leper by Matthew; and a Pharisee by Luke 7:39-40. The Pharisees were a group who tried to keep all the Mosaic Law. They were believers in the Supernatural and the Resurrection.

This Simon held a supper in his home and invited Jesus and his disciples to eat. Matthew Henry observes that Luke does not put this story in chronological sequence in his commentary on this passage. I looked carefully at the preceding journey of Jesus in Luke's seventh chapter, and traced his progress from Galilee south to Nain and then further south he was intercepted by a delegation of John the Baptist's disciples who heard the news of the raising of the widow's son. It is apparent that Luke chronicled the last journey to Jerusalem and then tells the story of Simon's Supper.

When we look at the details of the events surrounding this supper we see that this must be the same event recorded by Matthew, Mark, and John. Matthew puts this event just prior to the arrest and crucifixion. He identifies Simon as 'the leper' and puts the location in Bethany, just outside Jerusalem, and includes the story of the woman and the alabaster box of ointment (Matt. 26:6). This is significant, in so far as a leper was not allowed to mingle in company but was required to remain outside the town. There is only one conclusion; this man had been healed of leprosy.

Lazarus of Bethany, and his sisters, Martha and Mary are identified as present; Lazarus at the feast, Martha serving, and Mary coming in with the ointment. Mary's act of anointing Jesus is noted, and multiple voices of criticism are raised, Matt. 26:8, Mark 14:4 but interestingly John identifies the instigator of this as *Judas Iscariot* John 12:4-5.

Mary was the girl who had been a prostitute in the city, and found forgiveness and faith in Jesus. This was the girl Judas had grown up with, in the same small town of Bethany, just outside Jerusalem.

Jesus deals with Simon the Pharisee first, regarding the woman who was a known *Sinner* of the city. He makes it plain to Simon that grace and not the law apply to the repentant heart Lk.7:40-50. Luke tactfully omits her name and the location of the event, but says clearly she was a *Sinner*. The other Gospels tell her name and tactfully omit her past life history!

The primary work of Jesus was to effect reconciliation between us and our Father God. He paid the price on the Cross for all sin, and offers pardon even to a thief in his dying hour on the Cross. Simon the Leper, the righteous Pharisee, wants to work his way into Heaven by his deeds, but Jesus says there is forgiveness only after true repentance.

Who was Simon's son?

Now the outcry, instigated by Judas, reaches Jesus' ears; with some of the other disciples now taking part. He immediately turns to Judas and publicly rebukes him; in front of all at the dinner. John now picks up the story in his account with a very telling comment, and says: *"And supper being ended, the devil having now put into the heart of Judas Iscariot, Simon's son, to betray Him...."* John 13:2

Judas was not about to accept this rebuke of Jesus lightly, and John tells us that he went that same night to the chief priests of the temple and made his pact with hell; and set up the betrayal covenant for Thirty pieces of silver. Here is the secret that so many have never understood.

Judas was Simon's son!

He is rebuked publicly in front of his own father, in his home town where he grew up; and in front of many influential people from Jerusalem. Jesus has been saying that his kingdom is not of this world, that he was going to die, and Judas is now put down for his "wanting to help the poor". Jesus used a strong command in his language when he said to Judas, "Let her alone". In the original it is an imperative form of speech.

Let me interject here; whatever your past, when you place your faith and trust in Jesus, He will not allow others to harass you without dealing with them, in His own way and time. He is your Savior and Shepherd, your Rock and your Fortress!

So the up and coming young man, Simon's son, who doubtless had managed his father's estate while the father was a leper; who became treasurer to Jesus and the band of disciples; the man who John quietly says was a thief; makes his move to get rid of Jesus and get revenge for the *wrong* done him, and the loss of face in front of his father and his community.

The following night, Jesus and the 12 disciples hold their last supper in the upper room in Jerusalem; and Jesus tells Judas to go and do what he has to do. Judas departs, leaving some of the disciples thinking he was on an errand for the master.

Jesus then tells the rest of his followers that just as King David found his trusted friend Ahithophel to be a betrayer; so Judas is likened to Ahithophel, and he cites the verse in Psalm 41:9 quoted in John 13:18.

The parallels are fascinating as Judas was in a trusted inner circle as was Ahitophel. Both of them sought to advance their own standing, betrayed their leader, and committed suicide by hanging Matt. 27:5, 2 Sam. 17:23.

There is often a temptation in the life of a Christian to advance one's own cause at the expense of the plan and purpose of God. I had good friends who left the work of God for more 'profitable' occupations, sadly, at the expense of their own spiritual standing with the Lord who gave His all for us.

If you are a follower of Jesus, put His work first and He will take care of you Matt. 6:32-34. I have served the Lord for 64 years, and I have seen Him provide every time there was a need. He is faithful to those who put their trust in Him.

41 WHO WAS THE OTHER MARY?

D

o you like doing Crossword Puzzles? Then you will like unraveling this puzzle that few have bothered with. There are relationships here that the writers of the Gospels were familiar with, but if you do not know the connections, you miss a whole lot of the background to the early church in Jerusalem. By cross-referencing, we can find some startling answers. So read on and you will find it worth your time.

We first need to identify the known women at the Crucifixion, burial and Resurrection of Jesus, in order to properly understand who the 'Other Mary' really was. After the Crucifixion Luke tells us: *"The women who had been companions of Jesus from Galilee followed along. They saw the tomb where Jesus' body was placed."* Luke 23:55 The Message. The Evangelists each identify some of the women, and not always all the same ones.

Matthew lists three:

Mat 27:56 "among whom were Mary Magdalene, Mary the mother of James and Joses, and the mother of Zebedee's sons."

Mat 27:61 "And Mary Magdalene was there, and *the other Mary*, sitting opposite the tomb."

Mat 28:1 "Now after the Sabbath, as the first day of the week began to dawn, Mary Magdalene and *the other Mary* came to see the tomb." It is noteworthy that Matthew alone calls her the "Other Mary".

Mark observes these women:

Mar 15:40-41 "There were also women looking on from afar, among whom were Mary Magdalene, Mary the mother of James the Less and of Joses, and Salome, who also followed Him and ministered to Him when He was in Galilee, and many other women who came up with Him to Jerusalem."

Mar 15:47 "And Mary Magdalene and Mary the mother of Joses observed where He was laid."

Mar 16:1-2 "Now when the Sabbath was past, Mary Magdalene, Mary the mother of James, and Salome bought spices, that they might come and anoint Him. Very early in the morning, on the first day of the week, they came to the tomb when the sun had risen."

Luke mentions the following:

Luke 23:49 "But all His acquaintances, and the women who followed Him from Galilee, stood at a distance, watching these things."

Luke 23:55-56 "And the women who had come with Him from Galilee followed after, and they observed the tomb and how His body was laid. Then they returned and prepared spices and fragrant oils. And they rested on the Sabbath according to the commandment."

Luke 24:1"Now on the first day of the week, very early in the morning, they, *and certain other women with them*, came to the tomb bringing the spices which they had prepared."

Luke 24:9 "Then they returned from the tomb and told all these things to the eleven and to all the rest."

Luke 24:10 "It was Mary Magdalene, Joanna, Mary the mother of James, and the other women with them, who told these things to the apostles."

Finally we look at John's account:

John 19:25 "Now there stood by the cross of Jesus His mother, and His mother's sister, *Mary the wife of Clopas*, and Mary Magdalene."

John 20:1 "Now the first day of the week Mary Magdalene went to the tomb early, while it was still dark, and saw that the stone had been taken away from the tomb."

John 20:18 "Mary Magdalene came and told the disciples that she had seen the Lord,[2] and that He had spoken these things to her."

Listing the women mentioned by these Evangelists, we find:

Mary Mother of Jesus: Cited by John

Mary Magdalene: Cited by Matthew, Mark, Luke, John

Mary, mother of James & Joses: Cited by Matthew, Mark, Luke,

Mary, the wife of Clopas (Luke says Alphaeus Acts 1:13): Cited by John.

The other Mary: Cited by Matthew.

Now we have four possible Mary's mentioned.

First Mary, Jesus mother is always mentioned as such.

Second is Mary Magdalene who is always designated by her place of origin. Third is Mary; the mother of James the Less and Joses, and the fourth one, Mary the wife of Clopas. We clearly know who the first two are.

Let's look at #3 and #4.

Mary the mother of James the Less and Joses, and Mary the wife of Clopas.

Matthew identifies two Mary's in Matt 27:56, and says in verse 61 that Mary Magdalene and *the other Mary* sat watching the placement of Jesus body in the tomb. He has just mentioned Mary Magdalene and Mary mother of James the Less and Joses. Almost in the next breath he speaks of Mary Magdalene and the other Mary, now sitting down to watch the burial of Jesus in the tomb.

Matthew here seems to tie the Other Mary to his previous mention of the Mother of James and Joses. Her children are clearly known and mentioned as the sons of Alphaeus, Matt 10:3, Luke 6:15. John identifies this Mary, as the Sister of Jesus mother, and wife of Alphaeus in John 19:25. Alphaeus is mentioned several times in New Testament scripture.

The Hebrew form of this name is Cleophas, or Clopas according to Easton's Bible Dictionary. He is mentioned as having been with the Disciples on the day of the resurrection, and after hearing the tales of Jesus body missing from the tomb and the women telling of Angelic beings saying Jesus had come alive again, he leaves to journey home to Emmaus.

"Now behold, two of them were traveling that same day to a village called Emmaus, which was seven miles from Jerusalem." Luke 24:13

"Then the one whose name was Cleopas answered and said to Him, "Are you the only stranger in Jerusalem, and have you not known the things which happened there in these days?" Luke 24:18

We can clearly identify Cleopas [Alphaeus] as one of the followers of Jesus. His wife had been at the Cross and the empty Tomb, and was the 'other Mary' who was Jesus Aunt! Cleopas was thus actually Jesus' Uncle. When Jesus began his ministry He called a Tax Collector (a Publican), to be one of His disciples.

"As He passed by, He saw Levi the son of Alphaeus sitting at the tax office." And He said to him, "Follow Me." So he arose and followed Him." Mark 2:14. Levi was another name for Matthew the writer of the first Gospel. The conclusion is that *the other Mary* was Matthew's [Levi's] mother. Alphaeus [Cleophas] was her husband and father of James the Less, Levi later named Matthew and James, called 'not Iscariot'.

42 LUKE – THE DOCTOR IS IN!

There exists in the mind of many the idea that Doctors in the days of Jesus were untutored and lacked skill.

The truth is that many were learned men, who were even in those days learning to carry out delicate operations. Instruments have been found that were used for operating on the human skull, to lift a broken piece of bone and relieve pressure to the brain from an injury.

While much has been discovered today about hygiene and pain control, we need only to look at what has been found from archeology and the study of ancient writings, to understand that a respected doctor in the first century AD was usually a highly literate and qualified person.

Jerome refers to Doctor Lucas Medicus Antiochensis; that is Dr. Luke of Antioch. Certainly Luke, who traveled widely, writes in much detail of Antioch and seems to have spent some time there. It would seem that Luke traveled, probably by ship, from his home in Antioch to meet Paul in Troy. From there they traveled to Philippi, a major city of Macedonia, and a Roman Colony. Acts 16:8–12.

Paul the apostle mentions him in his letter to the Colossians 4:14 as Luke the Beloved Physician. In Luke's writings, (Luke and Acts) he makes use of specific medical terms for illnesses. His general writings speak much of his learning. Theologians who have studied Luke's writings comment on his scientific and historic accuracy, in his references to places and people. Disputed points that were used against Luke have in recent years been found to have been verified.

Souter suggests from the references in 2 Corinthians 8:18 and 12:18 that Luke may well have been the brother of Titus. Certainly we know that Luke became Paul's personal physician and close friend.

A careful reading of Luke's account of their shipwreck on the island of Malta would indicate that Luke practiced medicine, during their 3 month stay on the island. In Acts 28:8 we read of the Governor of the Island, Publius, whose father was dying of an advanced case of 'fever and dysentery' as the revised version accurately translates Luke's Greek text. This disease is still a problem in Malta and has many times been fatal there. Paul and Luke go to see him, and Luke diagnoses the disease, then steps aside as Paul lays hands on the old man and prays for instant healing. The people recognized this instantaneous miracle, and Luke uses the Greek word 'iaomai' that portrays the immediacy of the healing.

In the next verse, Luke speaks of many Islanders then approaching them, and of their being treated, and healed. Here the word Luke uses is 'therapeuo' which speaks of therapy, or treatment of diseases. He goes on to relate that the people 'tee-may', that is paid them for this medical treatment. So here we have a missionary doctor practicing medicine while Paul was actively praying and ministering the Word to the people. So successful was this partnership that when the winter was over, the populace supplied them with all they needed to journey on to Rome.

Paul in 2 Timothy 4:11 recounts the devotion and continued care of Luke for himself as he approached his execution. It is probable the Luke practiced medicine in Rome to support their needs, during the long time of Paul's imprisonment.

Sometimes we get to take care of and support a ministry leader; and thereby fill a much needed ministry opportunity for the Kingdom of God.

43 MOST EXCELLENT THEOPHILUS

Have you ever stopped to ask who Theophilus was? Let's see what the Bible can tell us about this man. When Dr. Luke wrote his 'Gospel' he began by preparing his reader to understand that the information he is sharing is from original sources, people whose stories have been verified.

Luke next says the purpose of this treatise is to help Theophilus understand that the things he already knew about Jesus; were now being written to amplify the knowledge he already possessed.

The name Theophilus means a 'friend of God' and is a distinctively Hebraic name.

In calling him 'Most Excellent' Luke is addressing a man of prominence. This form of address is applied to only two other people in the New Testament; they were the Governors Felix and Festus. It is not a greeting in the normal sense; but is used as a title when addressing a person in high office. So we are looking at a man who is prominent in a high office. Albert Barnes notes that *"these titles express no quality of the 'men,' but belong to the "office;" . . . even if their moral character be altogether unworthy of it."*

We therefore need to look around and see who this person might be and what his position may have been, that required his friend Dr. Luke to give him a verified account of the beliefs of the Christians.

Luke completed his greeting, and moves immediately to a discussion of things that pertain to events that occurred in the Temple at Jerusalem.

While Gentile Christians start with Jesus in Bethlehem, Luke begins with the Temple. This is significant and a possible indicator that the highly educated Dr. Luke of Antioch, Syria, as he is called by the earliest of the Church Fathers, was about to explain matters that were of significance to the Jewish Priests and Leaders.

In my view we are looking at the first presentation of a well-researched apologetic of the Story of Jesus, to a highly placed person, who must have been in contact with the Christians of his time. Those first years of the decade after the Crucifixion were years of rapid growth of the Christian Church in Jerusalem. There is ample evidence that they met in the Temple for most of their worship, and by 41 A.D. the Priests and the Sanhedrin were beginning to fear the power of the Jesus movement.

This might be a good time to ask ourselves, just when did Luke write his 'Gospel'?

There appears to be much uncertainty concerning the original date for the writing of Luke's Gospel. Obviously, from the context, it was written after the ascension of the Lord Jesus.

The murder of James the Brother of John the son of Zebedee, and shortly after that the arrest of Peter, who was miraculously delivered from prison by an Angel cf. Acts 12:25 occurred in 44 A.D. at the instigation of Herod Agrippa I, who had been given the territories formerly ruled by his grandfather, Herod the Great. Barnabas and other delegates from Antioch were there at that time in Jerusalem, with Paul, known as Rabbi Saul of Tarsus.

The High Priests succession is found in a listing by Josephus, the Jewish historian.

Caiaphas was the High Priest from 18–36 A.D. He was followed by Jonathan a son of Ananias, (the House of Annas, or Ananus) but only for about a year. He was removed from office because of atrocities he committed, and his brother was given the position of High Priest and ruled from 37 – 41 A.D.

This new High Priest was Theophilus, another son of Ananias. When Theophilus was installed as High Priest in 37 AD, one of the first acts of his administration was to give Saul of Tarsus letters to the Synagogues in Damascus to arrest Christians. Albert Barnes' notes on Acts 9:1-2 writes *"The high priest at that time was Theophilus, son of Ananus, who had been appointed at the feast of Pentecost, 37 a.d., by Vitellius, the Roman governor".*

Paul's dramatic Damascus Road conversion was undoubtedly reported to Theophilus by the accompanying soldiers, leaving the High Priest with questions that he needed answered. The records show that as a young man Theophilus was a student under Gamaliel, and with his brothers Jonathan and Simon, were classmates of Saul of Tarsus, and reputedly with Luke! It would make sense then that Theophilus would want to know more of the facts from someone who he had studied with; in the School of Gamaliel. Who better to ask than his former class-mate Dr. Luke?

That Luke wrote his 'Gospel' to this Theophilus the High Priest makes sense in time and place.

Luke ends his Gospel with the account of the resurrection of Jesus; and then suddenly moves to the account of two disciples walking to Emmaus. Luke pointedly names one of them as Cleopas. He points out that both Cleopas and Mary, his wife, recognized Jesus, and returned in the twilight to Jerusalem to inform the eleven of having seen Jesus alive.

Very significantly the last verses of Luke tell of the disciples seeing Jesus ascend, within eyesight of the Temple; and he ends with the Followers of Jesus returning to the Temple to continually worship there!

The entire thesis of Luke's Gospel opens and closes with reference to the Temple.

Luke writes of the 'Nazarenes' as they were first called, maintaining loyalty to the Temple and the Worship of Jehovah. Apparently written to the High Priest Theophilus, using his title, Most Excellent, it is significant that by the time Luke writes his story of the Acts, he does not use the title again, for by then Theophilus was no longer a High Priest. It is believed by several of the early Church Fathers that Theophilus became a follower of Jesus.

Reference sources: JFB and Adam Clarke's commentaries, Vines Word Studies, Josephus Ant., Dr. R. Mock 'High Priest of the Nazarene Ecclesia, Hugh Elton 'Jewish High Priests from Herod to the Destruction of the Temple.

44 JAMES, BISHOP OF JERUSALEM

Philip Shaff points out there are three theories concerning James.

"I would call them the brother-theory, the half-brother-theory, and the cousin-theory. Bishop Lightfoot (and Canon Farrar) calls them after their chief advocates, the Helvidian (an invidious designation), the Epiphanian, and the Hieronymian theories. The first is now confined to Protestants; the second is the Greek, the third the Roman view." -History of the Christian Church vol.1.Ch.4.

Which James was the Bishop of the Jerusalem Church?

I always begin my research by accepting the words of the Gospel writers as my primary source of information; before giving credence to writers of later generations.

There were three James' mentioned in the New Testament

1) James the brother of John, a son of Zebedee.

He was an apostle, and at the time of the famine predicted by Agabus; we are told that *"Now about that time Herod the king stretched forth his hands to vex certain of the church. And he killed James the brother of John with the sword".* *Acts 12:1-2* This happened circa 44 A.D.

2) James, the less, the son of Alpheus, is listed as an apostle of Jesus.

In Matt 10:2-5 the list includes a James, son of Alpheus. Mark and Luke corroborate this testimony. Alphaeus was the brother of Joseph, the husband of Mary. This James was thus a direct cousin of Jesus.

3) James a son of Mary, the mother of Jesus.

"Is not this the carpenter's son? Is not his mother called Mary, and his brethren, James, and Joses, and Simon, and Judas? And his sisters are they not all with us? Whence then hath this man all these things?" Mat 13:56

"And neither did his brethren believe in him." John 7:5

"When his family heard about it, they went to restrain him, because they kept saying, 'He's out of his mind!" Mark 3:21

One of Jesus' half-brothers is named James. That this James was not one of the apostles is clear from the context. Jesus himself says: *"A prophet is not without honor except in his own country and in his own house." Matt 13:57*

He is pointing out that even his brothers did not believe in him. Albert Barnes notes: *"The fair interpretation of this passage is that these were the sons and daughters of Joseph and Mary."*

Which James was the Bishop?

Around the time of Paul's return from his first missionary journey, 45 AD we read: *"And after they had held their peace, James answered, saying, Men and brethren, hearken unto me: . . . Wherefore my sentence is that we trouble not them, which from among the Gentiles are turned to God"* Acts 15:13; 19. James is giving a decision on behalf of the Jerusalem Church, and appears to be the leader.

In 58 AD Paul visited Jerusalem in company with Luke and Trophimus, an Ephesian. He again visited James, who was still alive and leading the Jerusalem Church.

"And when we were come to Jerusalem, the brethren received us gladly. And the day following Paul went in with us unto James; and all the elders were present" Acts 21:17-18. James was the prominent leader of the Church in Jerusalem at least from 45 to 62 A.D.

The Cultural use of the term 'brother'

The translation of 'brother' is from the Greek word 'adelphos' and is used to describe a near or remote relative cf. Strong's Greek dictionary. Westerners tend to use this in the narrow sense of born of the same father; the Middle East and African peoples use it in a much broader sense. This writer was born in Africa, and worked for 22 years with the African people. It is common usage to denote a man from your family or tribe, as a 'brother' even when he may be a second cousin, as I discovered many times.

Paul says that James the head of the Church was one of the original apostles of the Lord he wrote: *"But other of the apostles saw I none, save James, the Lord's brother' (Gal 1:19).*

The primary reference here is that James was an apostle. He talks of Jesus appearing to James, explicitly one of the apostles: *"After that, he was seen of James; then of all the apostles"* 1 Corinthians 15:7.

While none of the Evangelists record this fact, except Paul, it would seem that during his first meeting with James, Paul recounted his conversion experience of seeing Jesus on the Damascus road.

James seems then to have related his own experience of having seen Jesus after the resurrection. This would rule out James the son of Zebedee, who was at the time of that meeting dead by the hand of Herod.

It is no-where recorded that Jesus younger brothers became believers in him. If they had, there would have been much written about this. Jesus never appointed more apostles than the twelve. Only one other apostle was elected after Jesus death, Matthias who replaced Judas Iscariot. Acts 1:15-26.

The Biblical qualifications for Apostleship

The qualifications for an apostle of Jesus were clearly defined at the time. In Acts 1:22, an Apostle had to have been a witness of all that happened from Jesus' baptism in Jordan to his ascension to heaven. Jesus' earthly half-brother James would therefore not have qualified to be an apostle.

The James, who was the Apostle and Bishop of the Church in Jerusalem can therefore be no other than the Apostle James the less, the son of Alphaeus, a cousin of Jesus, appointed originally by Jesus as one of the original twelve apostles whom Jesus ordained to be his own.

45 THE EUNUCH OF ETHIOPIA

T he land of Ethiopia, also called Cush in Biblical times, encompassed the territory of what we now see as Ethiopia as well as Sudan and Somalia.

In the times of the Patriarchs there were historically recurring invasions by the two countries upon each other's territory. During the early life of Moses there was an ongoing war which was finally won by Moses as general of the Egyptian Army.

There are a few major references to Ethiopia found in Isaiah, 18:1, 20:3-4, and 45:14. The King of Ethiopia, Haile Selassie, claimed that the royal ancestry of the Kings of Ethiopia went back to King Solomon and the Queen of Sheba. Certainly there was a Semitic strain in the royal line. There is an interesting quotation in the International Standard Bible Encyclopedia that states:

"The Sabean inscriptions found in Abyssinia go back some 2,600 years and give a new value to the Bible references as well as to the constant claim of Josephus that the queen of Sheba was a "queen of Ethiopia."

In Ethiopia there were many African Jews, who claimed the God of Abraham, Isaac and Jacob as their God. I observed several Black Jews in Jerusalem in November 1966, all of them wearing the Kippah, and obviously Jewish in dress.

In the days of the early church, very shortly after Jesus had been raised from the dead and ascended to His father in Heaven, an important Ethiopian Government Official came to Jerusalem to Worship the God of Israel. The story of this event is recorded by Dr. Luke in Acts 8:26.

Here are some observations that I have concerning this story:

Firstly the story begins with a miraculous intervention in the ministry of Philip, who during the persecution of the church in Jerusalem had gone to the city of Samaria, and engaged in Revival meetings that were accompanied with signs and wonders. He is told by an Angel to leave immediately and go southwards along the road from Jerusalem to Gaza. This is Desert. He is not told why, but he knew enough to obey when God so ordered. Finally he is directed by the Spirit to approach the chariot carrying the Ethiopian Eunuch. Here are five things that give us understanding of this Ethiopian dignitary.

His Journey's purpose

We are told in the 27th verse that he had made the long journey for the purpose of coming to worship the God of Israel. Literally this involved coming to the Temple in Jerusalem to offer a sacrifice. This would have taken several weeks each way. For a man in his position as Minister of the Treasury of Ethiopia, this meant the expense of a long journey for not only himself but for his entire entourage. He was a Cabinet Minister to the Queen, and would never travel alone. Travel would likely be by boat and then overland using chariots. At the outset of this narrative, he is returning to his homeland.

His reception was proscribed

He finds that on arrival in Jerusalem, he has several strikes against him. First, he cannot actually enter the Temple. No Eunuch was permitted to enter the Temple. Second, he was a Gentile, and at best could have only entered the Court of the Gentiles, but that too was now unattainable. (Deut. 23:1; Lev.22:25) So he could not fulfill his objective; to worship God directly, as he had purposed.

His Understanding was perplexed

The rules and regulations of the Temple Worship perplexed him, but he procured a copy of the holy writings upon which so much of the religion was based. It was a copy of the book of the Prophet Isaiah, a book that would have taken a scribe a year to write. There were many detailed rules that were required of a scribe, to ensure that the book was perfectly copied from a master copy. It must have cost the Eunuch an enormous sum of money to purchase. Having invested a small fortune in this book, he commenced to read it as he traveled homewards. Again he is perplexed as he reads this book of Isaiah. He did not understand what the Prophet was saying. He desperately wishes for someone to unravel all this mystery.

His heart and mind were persuaded

God, who knew this man's heart, had already decided to intervene. Now God's man Philip was walking the road to Gaza; and the Spirit of God instructs him to join himself to this chariot. The Eunuch was reading aloud, as all the People of Jewish faith are instructed to do; and reading from Isaiah 53.

Acts 8:32-33 tells us what Philip heard the man read. This is a prophecy concerning the Judgment and Crucifixion of Jesus. Philip asks the Eunuch if he understands what he is reading, and is invited to explain this writing. Philip realized God had put him there in that place and time; to lead this hungry searching man to know the God of Israel and His Son, Jesus the Anointed One.

Believing in his heart what he hears, the Eunuch requests the Jewish rite of Mikvah. By the time Philip had explained the good news to the Eunuch, the chariot had reached the watered plain near Gaza, and there was the water needed for the new believer to make his 'Mikvah', being baptized by immersion in water in the name of Jesus. Philip asks for a spoken affirmation of his faith and upon hearing that he now believes Jesus is the Messiah, the prophetic fulfillment of Isaiah's writings, he promptly baptizes the Eunuch in the water.

He Proclaimed the Good News

The story concludes with the words, 'he went on his way rejoicing'. That was all the information Dr. Luke had when he wrote the Book of Acts.

Perhaps he went on reading and found Isaiah 56:3-5

"And do not let the eunuch say, Behold, I am a dry tree... I will give them an everlasting name that shall not be cut off."

This Eunuch returned to his land, and began to spread abroad the news that the awaited Messiah had come and fulfilled the Prophetic writings. Also that salvation was the gift of God to all who believe in and follow Jesus.

Others believed and for 2,000 years the Christian church flourished in Ethiopia. So the first Missionary to Africa seems to have been this dear African Convert to Christianity. Unknown to the outside world until the 18th century, believers proclaimed the message, because one man heard from God and left a revival to walk along a desert road.

Will you tell this story to someone God puts in your pathway? The outcome could be history making!

46 THE MAN FROM MACEDONIA

"There was a man of Macedonia standing, beseeching him, and saying, Come over into Macedonia, and help us." Acts 16:9

Paul decided to visit the churches he had planted on his first missionary journey; taking with him Silas as his companion (Acts 15:40). His initial purpose was to inform the gentile churches of the decision of the Jerusalem Council concerning the differences between the Jewish and gentile church practices. Paul recruited Timothy to his team while in Derbe & Lystra.

Paul was still looking for opportunities to further extend the reach of his ministry into new territories.

The Spirit of Jesus forbade him to go into the provinces of Asia and Bithynia (Acts 16:7). Seeking further guidance as to where to go next, they waited in the city of Troy. One night, Paul saw in a vision, a Macedonian man, standing and beseeching him to come to Macedonia. Luke, the writer of the book of Acts, indicates that he joined the party in Troy; using the word we in his first-hand account of what transpired. Paul shared his vision with the rest of the team and they came to a unanimous conclusion that this was a definite, God directed, commission (Acts 16:10).

Paul had seen this Macedonian man standing, and there was nothing hazy or vague about his vision.

The party immediately sought passage across the Aegean Sea to Macedonia. Paul's vision of this Macedonian man was burned into his memory; and he realized this was a defining moment for the fledgling Church. He would be planting the first Christian church in Europe, as we know it today. The port city of Neapolis hove into view, as they rounded the rocky headland that protected it; and finally the missionary group set foot in Europe for the first time.

Neapolis was a gateway to Philippi, about 10 miles inland from the port. They did not spend much time in Neapolis, but moved on quickly to Philippi, the chief city in the region.

This was a large and prosperous city, and also a Roman Colony in Greece. Paul was on a mission to find the man of his vision!

The account Luke writes here is a first-hand record of the events that transpired

It is significant to note that Paul meets Lydia at the Riverside Prayer group. She was a wealthy business woman, and became the first convert to Christ in Europe. After her conversion, Paul and the team accept her hospitality, but no significant man appears in the record. Paul and the team go to the Prayer place daily, and a slave girl fortune teller follows them, shouting out to all around that these men are Evangelists. This happened Luke says for many days. Paul became exasperated with this and finally one day he turned and cast out the demonic spirit from the girl. Her owners accused Paul and Silas, the obvious chief speakers, of treason against the Roman government! The magistrates reacted to this without verifying the facts, and had them severely beaten and jailed in the high-security portion of the prison. Up to this time there is still no account of the Macedonian man in the narrative.

With the Magistrates' imperious orders the jailer shoves Paul and Silas into the inner prison and clamps their feet in the stocks; limiting their ability even further to escape. Now the unaccountable happens. Bleeding, hurting and wrongly imprisoned, Paul and Silas get happy! They begin to sing, and praise God, they are excited about something, and keep up the prayers and praise until midnight. An earthquake interrupts their joy and exultation, and they find themselves free of their bonds.

I have to ask myself; what on earth are they so happy about?

The only logical answer is that they have finally met the man they have been looking for! When the Philippian Jailer attended to their incarceration, Paul recognized him as the man from his vision in Troy. Here was the man who said 'Come over into Macedonia and help us' in Paul's vision. Days had passed and finally they recognized the man; and realized that as Paul later wrote to the Romans, 'All things work together for good to them that love God' (Romans 8:28). The earthquake was the tipping point in this experience.

Paul took charge of the prisoners, and when the jailer arrived on the scene, Paul told him not to commit suicide, for they were all safely there. Having looked death in the face at that moment, the jailer became conscious of his need of salvation, and asked Paul and Silas what he should do to be saved. His conversion translated into compassion, and Luke recounts the scene in the jailer's house, where he personally applied first-aid to the Evangelist's wounds.

The account of the events in Philippi closes with the humiliated magistrates apologizing to Paul and Silas, and the departure of these two from the city. It is very much the purpose of Luke to show that the early believers preached the scriptural truths concerning Jesus; but they depended heavily upon the direction of the Holy Spirit for guidance in their activities and projected ministry outreaches.

God is still in the business of giving guidance to those who are committed to His purposes; those who have determined to make Jesus known to lost and needy people in the nations of the world today.

47 THE MOTHER OF RUFUS

In the days of the early church, when a heathen professor in Antioch, heard of Anthusa, a Godly woman; the mother of Chrysostom, he threw up his hands and cried, *"What woman, these Christians have!"*

In the closing chapter of the book of Romans Paul pays tribute to one who evidently had proved herself to be a veritable 'mother in Israel' to him personally. Paul writes in Romans16: 13 LNT: *"Greet Rufus for me, whom the Lord picked out to be his very own; and also his dear mother who has been such a mother to me".*

Nearly 30 years had passed since Paul's conversion to Christ. He had traveled in many parts of Europe. Now he's heading back to Jerusalem, with the offering of the Gentiles, to attend the feast of Pentecost. Paul has a long memory for old friends and as he writes his letter to Rome, he remembers some who are now living there and mentions Rufus, and his mother. Paul refers to Rufus, as the Lord's hand-picked one; clearly Paul knew Rufus very well.

At the time of Paul's conversion to Christianity in Damascus, Paul suffered persecution and barely escaped with his life. He proceeded to Jerusalem, and after a cautious acceptance by the church, began to fearlessly proclaim Jesus as savior to the Jews. Massive persecution broke out, and the Christians in Jerusalem conducted Paul to the coast, and sent him to his hometown of Tarsus. Paul had lost all his friends, was on his own, and probably lonely; and I'm sure disheartened. He had sacrificed his all for the gospel.

Due to this persecution of the Church in Judea, many believers fled to other places

After the martyrdom of Stephen, the Christians were scattered; and some fled to Antioch and began to preach Jesus to the Greeks there. Many Greeks believed, and a congregation sprang up in that place Acts 11:20-21.

A great turning to the Lord took place in the city, and Barnabas was sent there to investigate this revival that was occurring. He realized that this was a place where 'Rabbi Saul', known later as Paul to the Greeks and Romans, would fit in very well. Barnabas traveled on to Tarsus, searched for Paul, and brought him to Antioch.

Among the leadership in Antioch was one Simon, who was called Niger, the Black man. LNT. He is mentioned in connection with Lucius also of Cyrene, and included with Paul and Barnabas as being prophets and teachers in the Church Acts 13:1. According to early church tradition this is the same Simon who carried the Cross of Jesus. In Simon's house, Paul found a refuge when he was brought to Antioch from Tarsus. Now, years later, Paul has many friends, better friends, but he still has a long memory for Rufus and his mother who were among the first to welcome him when he was brought to Antioch.

Now who is she?

Her name is never mentioned, possibly just a simple woman. On the surface there seems to be nothing outstanding about her. She was not like Priscilla, appearing to overshadow her husband, or like Lydia, who seems to have an aptitude for business. She was just a homebody; serving Jesus in the daily round and the common task, yet hers is a story worth hearing.

This nameless woman mothered Paul; until under her healing influence he found himself again. Paul never forgot that blessed ministry, that big heart, that soft voice, that kindly face. I'm sure there were many nights that Rufus and Paul sat down and talked, discussing the promises of God; and around about them was that mother's sweet presence and influence.

Rufus and his mother and father were well known to the church

Mark speaks of *Simon of Cyrene* coming in from the country, some translations say 'from the fields', and adds that he was *the father of Alexander and Rufus* Mark 15:21.

Now Rufus' father, Simon was present at the Passover, when Jesus was crucified. Simon was the man who carried Jesus Cross on the way to Calvary. He was a black man, called 'niger', from the country of Libya and the city of Cyrene; that area today is called Tripoli, in North Africa. Simon had immigrated to Palestine, and was living in Jerusalem; there were a number of Cyrenian Jews known to be living there Acts 6:9; 11:19.

162

What a record this family created for itself

The father carried Jesus Cross; the mother proved her devotion to Jesus by ministering to the Lords apostle in his time of need. Who knows what the world and in particular the Church, owes to that consecrated African Mother?

Privileged? She may not have recognized it at the time but yes, a thousand times yes! When every door was shut she opened hers and ministered to his needs. She cared and loved, as only a mother can. She preached the gospel by deeds. Her daily walk told whose she was and who she served.

And what was her reward? The boys grew up to be men who loved and followed Jesus; and we find Rufus, and his mother, serving and in fellowship with the church in Rome some 30 years later. It all began in Antioch where the believers were first called "Christians" Acts 11:26.

How many of us, recognize our privilege in opportunity; and rise to the occasion? Mother, don't lament your lack of opportunity to serve God in your home; you never know what the future holds.

Dr. Campbell Morgan writes in his biography, that he had four sons; and all of them grew up to become really great preachers, like their dad. One day as the family was gathered together, the youngest son, Howard asked, *"Dad, Who is the greatest preacher in this family?"* Dr. Campbell Morgan looked at each of them in turn and then, with a twinkle in his eye, said *"Your Mother!"*

Mothers, honor your opportunities, accept your responsibilities, and radiate the light of the gospel of Jesus Christ from your kitchen. Study the story of the mother of Rufus. See how the humblest of duties can be transformed into services as splendid as an Angel. Children are not encumbrances, but lives in the making, which will carry remembrances of your home with them throughout their future. Paul remembered that atmosphere of heaven, and still dreamed of sweet fellowship over thirty years later.

48 APOLLOS - INTEGRITY TESTED

A uthor Richard Exely said: *"Adversity tests Character, but Success tests Integrity".* I studied for several years under Mrs. Mary Eason, a leading teacher in Child Evangelism Fellowship, and in her lectures she would often break in with an "Oh, by the way!" Those little anecdotes taught me more sometimes than the whole lecture.

Every now and then there appears in the Bible an: "Oh, by the way!" and the introduction of this man in the book of Acts 18:24-28 is one of those special incidents.

The Jew with a Gentile name!

'*And a certain Jew named Apollos, born at Alexandria . . .*' Acts 18:24. His name is Greek, though he was a Jew, not only by religion, but by birth. It seems strange at first glance that we should find a Jew, not only with a Roman name, as Aquila, an eagle; but with the name of one of the false gods, as Apollos or Apollo in the text.

In Dake's annotated bible, he explains that Apollos is the shortened form of Apollonius. There was an Apollonius of Rhodes, a Greek poet, born in Alexandria, Egypt some 200 years before the time of the book of Acts. Apollonius cultivated epic poetry in the grand style of Homer. Apollonius's most important and only extant work is the epic poem Argonautica. This Apollonius was an important literary influence on Virgil. I would hazard a guess that his parents named him Apollos after the man born in Alexandria; but called Apollonius of Rhodes.

Born at Alexandria

This was a celebrated city of Egypt, built by Alexander the Great, from whom it took its name. It was seated on the Mediterranean Sea, about twelve miles west of the Canopic branch of the Nile. Here too was the Lighthouse of Pharos, one of the Seven Wonders of the World.

It was in this city that Ptolemy Soter founded the famous academy called the Museum, in which a society of learned men devoted themselves to philosophical studies. Some of the most celebrated schools of antiquity flourished here; great numbers of Jews were in this place; here too lived Philo the famous Jewish philosopher. Nowhere was there such a fusion of Greek, Jewish, and Oriental peculiarities; and an intelligent Jew educated in that city could hardly fail to manifest all these elements the Scripture mentions of his mental character.

He was eloquent

He turned his Alexandrian culture to high account, and became mighty in the scriptures. His eloquence enabled him to express clearly and enforce skillfully what, as a Jew, he had gathered from a diligent study of the Old Testament Scriptures. "Vincent's Word Studies" suggest that he *"came to Ephesus after the departure of the Apostle Paul, and while Aquila and Priscilla were there; the reason of his coming was to preach the Word, as he did".*

He spoke boldly in the synagogue

Although he did not know as yet that Jesus of Nazareth was the Messiah he preached what he knew. Aquila and Priscilla took him aside and instructed him more perfectly in "the way of God", i.e., in the knowledge of Christ Acts 18:26.

He then proceeded to Corinth, where he met Paul Acts 18:27; 19:1. He was there very useful in watering the good seed Paul had sown 1Cor 1:12, and in gaining many to Christ. His disciples were much attached to him 1Cor 3:4-7, 22, and were attracted by his rhetorical style acquired in Alexandria, as contrasted with Paul's lack of "excellency of speech and enticing words of man's wisdom" 1Cor 2:1-4, and even in their estimation Paul's "contemptible speech" 2 Cor 10:10.

Some at Corinth abused his name, turning it into a party watchword

They were saying, "I am of Apollos," so popular was he. But Paul, while condemning their party spirit, commends Apollos, and writes that he had "greatly desired our brother Apollos to come unto you" Corinthians 1Cor 16:12. Apollos was disinclined to come at that time; probably to give no handle for party zeal, until the danger of it should have passed away.

Jerome states that Apollos remained at Crete until he heard that the divisions at Corinth had been healed by Paul's epistle; then he went and became bishop there.

Apollos' main excellence was as builder-up, rather than a founder, of churches. His humility in submitting, with all his learning, to the teaching of Aquila and even of Priscilla (a woman), speaks well for him.

166

His fervency and his power in Scripture, and his determination to stay away from where his well-deserved popularity might be made a handle for party zeal, are all fine traits in his Christian character.

Here I believe is the ultimate bond of Christians

Love that avoids division, and is ready to learn from one another, is the glue of unity in a church. I hope you will be challenged, as I was in studying this man's example, to work for unity among believers in the Lord Jesus Christ. The last Bible notice of Apollos is in Titus 3:13, where Paul charges Titus, then in Crete: *"Bring Zenas the lawyer and Apollos on their way diligently, that nothing may be wanting to them."*

What a testimony to a man of peace.

49 TROPHIMUS PRAISED IN THE CHURCHES

fter the uproar had ceased'. This is how the 20ᵗʰ chapter of the Book of Acts begins. Exciting events had taken place in Ephesus, which Luke recounts in Acts 19. After two years of ministry to Jews and Greeks in Ephesus, a riot broke out and it was prudent that Paul leave town for a while. Paul decided to extend their missionary journey into Macedonia and Greece.

In Acts 20:4, Luke says that Paul after going to Macedonia and Greece returned via Macedonia to Asia. Dr. Luke of course traveled with Paul; and he names the other seven men who accompanied them on this trip. Their journey took several months. They were in Greece for 3 months and before that they had traveled all over Macedonia as well. The journey from Ephesus to Troy and Miletus are included in the story.

One of these men was Trophimus, first mentioned by name here, he was from the Roman province of Asia.

In Acts 21:29 he is specifically called an Ephesian. His name *Trophimus* means 'Adopted' or 'Foster Child'. He was a Greek living in Ephesus, who came to faith in Christ through Paul's preaching and teaching, which continued there for about 2 years.

When Paul received a letter from the Church at Corinth in Greece, he was deeply disturbed at the account of the events taking place there. He responded to them with his second letter to the Corinthians, written from Ephesus. The first letter had outlined strong disciplinary measures the Church should take to bring an offending Christian to repentance.

This second letter was to ensure forgiveness and acceptance by the Church, since the offender had truly shown the fruits of his repentance. This was so important that Paul sought out dependable messengers to carry this letter and confirm his instructions. Titus and Trophimus were the men Paul entrusted to carry this Second Epistle to the Corinthians.

Trophimus was a member of the Ephesian church, whom Paul had found reliable.

Second Corinthians 8:16-24 specifically mentions that the person referred to was one of Paul's 'Traveling Companions'. A process of elimination, among the 8 traveling companions of Paul, leads me to the conclusion that the trusted and highly esteemed brother, who had Paul's full confidence, was Trophimus.

The Church at Ephesus later contributed to the offering for the poor in Jerusalem; and sent delegates along with Paul to see the gift reached the church in Jerusalem, and one of those delegates was Trophimus 1 Cor. 16:1-3. During Paul's defense in Caesarea before Governor Felix, he makes the statement that his last missionary journey was to bring offerings for the poor to Jerusalem Acts 24:17.

We also learn from the narrative that Trophimus accompanied Paul to Rome and traveled with him after his release from his first imprisonment. At one point in their travels, Trophimus became very ill and Paul in his last written letter, 2 Tim 4:20, says he left him at Miletus. This was not far from his home city of Ephesus, and there were friends and family nearby who were able to take care of him, and get him back home after his recovery.

The Jews from Asia assumed Paul brought Trophimus into the Temple in Jerusalem.

The Temple had an outer court called the 'Court of the Gentiles' and there was a partition, or wall, with notices warning Gentiles that the next area was for Jews only, and that any Gentile entering that part of the Temple would be stoned to death. Tertullus the Lawyer, when accusing Paul, repeated the accusation involving Trophimus during the hearing in Caesarea cf. Acts 24:6. Luke makes is very clear however that Trophimus never entered the temple Acts 21:29.

Trophimus is one of many, barely noticed, heroes of the "Early Church", who traveled and assisted Paul in his ministry for several years, and finally, tradition tells us, he was beheaded by the Roman Emperor Nero.

Research resources include: The International Standard Bible Encyclopedia, Easton's Bible Dictionary and Adam Clarke's commentary.

50 DEMETRIUS THE SILVERSMITH

"Wherefore if Demetrius, and the craftsmen which are with him, have a matter against any man, the law is open, and there are deputies: let them implead one another"
Act 19:38.

Demetrius of Ephesus, the leader of the Silversmiths Guild was influential and wealthy

The guild of Silversmiths was employed in creating miniature shrines or 'naoi'; models of the temple, and the goddess. These were sold at enormous profit to the thousands of pilgrims who visited the site. The artisans, whose trade depended on the sale of clay, wood and silver artifacts resembling the goddess and the shrine of Diana, were experiencing a recession.

Demetrius called a meeting of all the tradesmen, and made a presentation of the facts as he saw them: Acts 19:25-28.

Our trade has enriched us. Paul has persuaded people all around Asia to turn from our god. Our livelihood is endangered. The temple is in danger of being made of no account. The goddess Diana could be deposed from her magnificent worship.

Demetrius whipped the crowd into a frenzy; acclamation turned to chanting and then morphed into a full scale riot!

The violent riot Demetrius incited, threatened the lives of Paul and his followers

It was into this society that Paul the Apostle had come in 51 A.D. and the Christian church had flourished in Ephesus and its surroundings during the next three years. Many of the new believers were still in possession of the books of witchcraft that was part of their old life, reputedly worth around $10,000 U.S. Dollars (JFB Commentary).

These they burned in a huge bonfire celebration as testimony of their new found faith in Jesus.

The rapid spread of Christianity made a noticeable impact on Ephesus, and its environs, both spiritually and materially. Demetrius instigated the riot in an attempt to get rid of Paul and the Christians. It also put the city officials in danger of an Inquiry from Rome! The city clerk advised they take the matter up in court if they had an accusation against Paul or the Christians.

It was this riot that caused Paul to leave Ephesus; and move back to Macedonia and Greece.

Before leaving Paul appointed Timothy to pastor the Ephesian Church. Later Paul sent Tychicus to replace Timothy 1 Tim1:3; 2 Tim 4:12. The ministry to the people of Ephesus continued, and finally the apostle John, the son of Zebedee, came to pastor the church; and oversee the work in Asia and Greece, subsequent for Paul's imprisonment.

Sometime between 54 and 62 A.D. a conversion took place that must have made the inhabitants of Ephesus sit up and take notice. Newspaper headlines could have read:

"Silversmith Guild President converts to Christianity!" Demetrius, the wealthy and influential leader of the riot, had become a follower of the Lord Jesus Christ. He was discipled in the faith and proved himself to be a real Christian. John the aged apostle was the Pastor of the church in Ephesus when he wrote to Paul's former traveling companion, Gaius in Corinth, saying:

"Demetrius has received a good report from everyone, and is doctrinally sound. I can testify to this personally, and you know I tell the truth!" -Author's transliteration of 3 John vs12.

When Demetrius found Christ, his conduct proved it. Faith without works is dead!

51 DRUSILLA THE BEAUTIFUL

Herod Agrippa the First, son of Herod the Great, looked down with pride at his new-born baby girl. She was unusually beautiful and dewy-eyed, so Herod named her Drusilla, meaning watered by the dew. Born about A.D. 37, she became an even more beautiful young woman. Her siblings were Herod Agrippa II, Mariamne and Bernice. The two older sisters, also beautiful, were insanely jealous of Drusilla's unusual haunting beauty.

Agrippa I betrothed Drusilla, at age six, to Prince Callinicus; a descendant of Antiochus Epiphanes. The betrothal was annulled when Callinicus did not fulfill the pre-marriage contract; so Agrippa gave her in marriage at the tender age of 14 to King Azizus of Emesa. His Kingdom encompassed most of the Bekaa Valley; where the ruins of the Temple to the Sun God are still to be seen at Baalbek. This territory, now known as Lebanon, was then under the control of Rome.

Felix the procurator of Judea from A. D. 53-60 first laid eyes on the young and beautiful 16 year old Drusilla while on a visit to King Azizus. Felix fell madly in love with her and determined to have her. He employed a friend, Simon, to persuade Drusilla to desert the cruel King Azizus, and become Felix' wife. Drusilla, married Antoninus Felix the Procurator in A.D. 54, and became interested in her Jewish heritage; with its expectation of a coming Messiah. In 58 A.D. Paul, the apostle, was brought as a prisoner to Felix' Palace in Caesarea. Drusilla, now 21 years of age, asked Felix to arrange a meeting with Paul. Felix knew quite a bit about the Christians, but Drusilla wanted to hear Paul explain the faith in Christ.

Felix was agreeable as he wished to know more about the Christians; and felt they could talk more freely with Paul in private, than in open court. When Paul began talking to them, he already knew their history; so instead of talking about the doctrine and differences between Judaism and Christianity, he reasoned with Felix and Drusilla on three subjects. Righteousness, Self-Control, and Judgment to come! Josephus notes, Drusilla was living in adultery with Felix, and this was probably the reason why Paul dwelt in his discourse before Felix particularly on Self-Control. St. Luke tells us in Acts 24:25 that Felix trembled.

Historians note that Felix had been married twice before this

He was both drawn to the subject; and horrified at the possible consequences of his past life. The last verses of Acts 24 tell of his frequent meetings with Paul, hoping for a bribe to set Paul free; repeatedly listening to what Paul preached.

Matthew Henry observes, *"Many are fond of new notions and speculations in religion, and can hear and speak of them with pleasure, who yet hate to come under the power and influence of religion: [they] can be content to have their judgments informed; but not their lives reformed."*

Two years into Paul's detention, Felix was replaced by Porcius Festus. Felix did what so many politicians do. He left Paul's fate in the hands of the new incoming governor Festus, to please the Jews.

Antoninus Felix and Drusilla went to live in Pompey, Italy for the next 17 years

This was home to many Roman aristocrats, including Caesar. The city was situated at the foot of Mount Vesuvius, with a beautiful view of the bay, and boasted many magnificent homes and public buildings, including a temple where Caesar worshiped when in residence there.

One day, without warning, the volcano came to life, spewing out molten lava and a deadly gas that covered the city in a matter of moments Soldiers standing guard were instantly killed by the gas, and their bodies covered with the molten lava.

Drusilla, and her son Agrippa, by Felix, were consumed in the horrible eruption of Mount Vesuvius, in A.D. 79 which destroyed Pompey. Sadly there is no record of this beautiful woman, who personally listened to Paul the apostle, or her husband Felix, ever coming to the knowledge of Christ as their Savior.

For some people, the longest journey is the journey from the head to the heart; those who have taken it have never regretted doing so.

The End.

ABOUT THE AUTHOR

Jim Cole-Rous was born in Cape Town, South Africa. He studied at the South African Bible Institute and served as an Ordained Minister and Missionary for 22 years in Africa.

He ministered in 14 countries in Africa, successfully planting 5 new congregations in Southern Africa. He served on the National Board with Mission Aviation Fellowship of South Africa, and as CEO of MAF-Transkei. Jim is widely traveled, having been in Portugal, Greece, Lebanon, Syria, Jordan and Israel.

While working with MAF in Transkei as a Pilot, Jim also taught Hermeneutics, Bible Manners and Customs and New Testament Survey at the Transkei Bible College in Umtata. In 1978 Jim moved to the U.S.A. where he obtained his degree in Aerospace Maintenance Technology, then returned to serve in Pastoral and Evangelistic work.

It was after this that he began writing seriously, doing research in Theology and Ancient History. In 2007 Jim was asked to help with the formation of Network 211, to reach 10 Million people with the Gospel on the Internet in 10 years.

Jim Cole-Rous is currently Director of Content and Publisher for Network211.com and Managing Editor for the Ozarks Chapter Newsletter of American Christian Writers.

He has over 200 non-fiction articles published; and is busy with his second book, the life story of a dedicated missionary, 'Rowena – The Girl Who Wouldn't Quit', due for publication in early 2014.

Jim resides in Springfield MO, is father to a son, a daughter, and four grandchildren. He enjoys playing golf and listening to classical music.

INTENTIONALLY LEFT BLANK

CPSIA information can be obtained at www.ICGtesting.com
Printed in the USA
LVOW05s1654190814

399893LV00011BA/190/P